The Meaning of
meow

Understanding and Caring for Your Cat

Editor: Karyn Gerhard

Illustrator: Dee Densmore D'Amico

Design: NICI von Alvensleben

A LifeTime Media Production

LifeTime Media, Inc.

352 Seventh Avenue

New York, NY 10001

www.lifetimemedia.com

For all domestic and foreign rights information and sales,
please contact LifeTime Media, Inc. at
212-631-7524 or sales@lifetimemedia.com

The Meaning of
mɛow

Understanding and Caring for Your Cat

DIANA JESSIE

Foreword by Cat Cora

Table of Contents

Foreword

Some people may wonder, why is a chef writing a fore-word for a book on cats? It can't just be the coincidence of her first name!

Well, it's not. As funny as it sounds, Meow Mix and I have been doing the same thing for years—just for different customers.

Food is not only my profession, it is my passion. I come from a family where cooking and eating were the center of our lives. From an early age I have been obsessed with combining of the freshest meats, poultry, fish, and veg-etables to create delicious meals that satisfy.

For thirty years, Meow Mix has had the same passion— using the freshest ingredients to create a food that cats would ask for by name. From flavorful morsels of dry food to wet food in every flavor imaginable to delectable treats, they have become experts in what makes a cat purr.

Although proper nutrition is the cornerstone for a healthy kitty, giving them the right food is only one small part of being a cat owner. Meow Mix believes that in order to be a great cat owner you must truly understand your feline, which is why they have put together this information and fun book. In these pages you will find out not only how to choose the right cat for your household, what items you will need to make your feline happy, and how to keep her healthy, you will learn how to think like a cat. From understanding what they are saying with a flick of their tail, to figuring out when kitty is telling you she is sick, to understanding their fascination with the plastic bags, this book has it all. Reading this book will help you understand how the cat sees her world, and how she sees you. And a well-cared-for cat will give you happiness and joy from tiny kittenhood to adult.

So, make yourself a nice piece of salmon, give your kitty some of her own, and enjoy learning how to think like a cat! Remember, it all starts with "Meow."

—Cat Cora

A Bit of Cat Background

You've fallen for those cute, furry, four-legged creatures of the feline persuasion. But what do you really know about them? If you're like most people, you didn't get beyond the winsome meow or the sensuous rub against your leg. The real deal maker was the body-consuming vibration called purring. But is that enough to make you bring one into your home?

A Brief History of Cats

According to anthropologists, cats probably evolved in the desert-like conditions of North Africa. They chewed on plants for moisture and ate anything that was foolish enough to move or come within sniffing distance. Cats didn't walk in others' paw prints; unlike canines, they didn't need to be part of a gang. They could be social or solitary without making a big deal of it.

From the earliest times, it has been clear that cats are keen observers and logical thinkers. They saw that humans collected food and stored it for future use, which invited all types of creatures to help themselves to the convenient food supply. It made sense to the cat to take up residence close to humans and avail themselves of the ready-made hunting ground that had been created. Get close to your primary target and then you have more time for important things such as napping.

Cats initially endeared themselves to humans by controlling the rodent population and protecting the food supply, but as they made a place for themselves in the human household, they discovered other benefits. Their natural voice of contentment, purring, had a positive effect on humans and in return, humans offered special gifts to cats in the form of warm hearths, tidbits of caught and dressed meat, and laps. Cats soon discovered they not only had a home, but they were in control.

Cats made a few mistakes in their campaign to have human company. They discovered that humans would share their food, but were not eager to share what cats contributed to the larder. Clearly, mice and rats were not choice items, especially live ones. Another discovery was that there were certain people who were not well-positioned in the community. Being the choice pet of kings, emperors, and the like was fairly secure as long as subjects understood that cats were protected. But being associated with people who rode broomsticks and cooked in large caldrons often led to serious consequences. Black cats in particular were subject to perilous times. Farm cats loved the warm barns and haystacks frequented by field mice, but did not find the little boys grabbing them by the tail suitable companions.

Assumptions—FACT VS. FICTION

Owners of canines and other types of pets—birds, goldfish, or pigs—are quick to question the choice of a cat as a pet. This is mostly due to numerous misguided assumptions. Here are some assumptions that always come up in this discussion.

Cats are aloof FICTION

Have you ever tried to keep a cat off your lap when you're reading? Or tried to sleep when the cat wants to play? Or tried to sneak a piece of turkey out of the refrigerator for a midnight snack without sharing it with the cat? Cats are not aloof. They observe the actions of humans and determine which of those actions have appeal or is worthwhile. If some human action bores a cat, the cat will take a nap or find something more entertaining to suggest to the human.

Cats are independent FICTION

Cats enjoy the company of friends but they don't require it. They like humans who are considerate and appreciative of a cat's uniqueness. They aren't particularly thrilled with loud noises, fighting, or the mail carrier; but they don't bark, chase, or bite to demonstrate their displeasure—they just walk away or go back to sleep.

Assuming that a cat is independent and should be left to fend for itself is the most serious of errors. Cats will simply seek out more comfortable accommodations, better food, and more attentive humans. Why should a cat stay where it is unappreciated?

Cats are fastidious FACT

Cats are are organized and occasionally anal about their routine. When humans begin to ignore regular activities—feeding time, play time, and nap time—cats simply refuse to go along with the chaos. Sometimes humans think they need to reorganize their life which automatically makes a feline nervous. They move furniture as a pastime. They think nothing of moving the cat's litter box or the cat's dishes; these decisions are made without discussion. There are even times when humans do unthinkable things such as bringing strangers into the house. Cats can be flexible, but they appreciate an opportunity to adjust to change. When a cat does not want to participate, she will leave the room. If you move the couch from the spot where it is sunny every morning, the cat will find another sunny spot without consultation, even if it is in the middle of the sink. When the cat bites your fingers, she is only reminding you that as a kitten you always let her bite your fingers.

If you have a habit of getting up and leaving the bed unmade, the cat has always counted on having your warm spot for an hour or two. Buying a futon bed or installing a Murphy bed is not part of the cat's plan. The consequences are not the cat's fault. When you install guests in the cat's room, there is a practice known as middening (leaving feces uncovered, often in a surprise location) that might cause the guests to leave. Work with the cat and be sure there are alternatives; otherwise the cat could become even more anal.

Cats are picky FICTION

The notion that cats are picky usually arises out of the fact that unwanted changes have been made in their routine. Unlike humans, cats actually do not prefer variety— if you change their food, litter, or surroundings, expect objections or boycotts! It is not in a cat's nature to be picky, but constantly changing their food will turn them

into finicky eaters. Cats certainly will not starve if you change the food, but they may become very unhappy.

It is the same with litter. You change to clumping litter because it is easier to maintain, but the cat liked the old litter because it was very friable and easy to throw. The litter box serves an important function; it is unwise to change something that works, and the consequences could get messy. And that grungy catnip mouse that you put in the trash at least twice a week—somehow it always seems to magically reappear. If your cat is fond of something, or used to the old ways, there is nothing to be gained by making a to change unless health and safety are at issue.

So remember, only you can create a picky cat!

A Cat's-Eye View

Clyde the cat answers your questions about

FOOD AND WATER

DEAR CLYDE,
I put out fresh water for my Louie every day but he insists on sitting in the sink and drinking from the dripping faucet, or from the toilet. Why won't he drink from his own bowl?

Have you ever tasted water that's been sitting around for a while? It tastes funky and stale, no doubt about it. We like fresh water, just like you do! We also like the sight and sound of running water, which is probably why Louie is fascinated with the toilet (some of my friends will even put their paw in their dish and drag it around, just to watch the water move!).

Plastic dishes can hold some nasty smells—it's best to use stainless steel. We also hate getting our whiskers wet, so if he's got to dunk his face in the bowl, he'll stay away.

I really like the water bowl I have here—it's a dish that is also a working fountain! It keeps the water moving so tastes fresh, and I love to watch the little waterfall. You can get one for Louie at any pet store.

CHAPTER 2

- ✦ WHY Do You Want a Cat?

- ✦ IS Everyone Prepared to be a Cat Staffer?

- ✦ CAN You Afford a Cat?

- ✦ DO You Have Space for a Cat?

Are You Cat Staff Material?

When you start looking for the right pet, there are many things to consider—how it will fit into your life, how you will interact with it, how much time it will require, and the cost of caring for it, among them. From the outset, your life with a cat will be quite different from the life you might have with a dog—dogs have owners, and cats have staff. Here are some questions to ask before taking the plunge.

Why Do You Want a Cat?

Some people want a beautiful, purebred show cat because they are predictable in following breed traits. Some people are influenced by a friend who has a long-haired cat, so they want a long-haired cat. Some people want a cat because they feel their home is not complete without a pet, or they want a companion for their children. Some people are just pushovers and cannot say no to kittens. The best reason to bring a cat into your household is that it makes you feel good, and when that happens, there is likely to be reciprocity. A cat can help reduce stress in your life, and you can do the same for your cat.

There are dozens of good reasons to want to bring a pet into your household, but there are also some bad ones. The worst reason to get a cat is as a gift for someone who

is not expecting an animal. A cat is a lot of responsibility, and giving it to someone who is not ready for that responsibility could end up in the pet being neglected or abandoned. (It is for this reason that many shelters will not allow adoption around holidays such as Christmas or Halloween, when people just want a black cat for affect and not as a permanent pet).

Whatever the reason, the bottom line is that you are willing to take on the responsibility of being a pet owner. People sometimes make the assumption that cats require less attention and less care, but nothing could be further from the truth. A cat has needs and demands that cannot be ignored, but making the cat feel good by keeping it healthy, well fed, secure and loved is perfect payback for that cat that always cuddles, purrs like a well tuned jaguar, and appears at the sound of your voice.

Is Everyone Prepared to Be a Cat Staffer?

If you live with other people, are they all agreed on getting a cat? Before bringing home a cat, you must discuss it with everyone living in the house, and the decision must be unanimous. A cat will sense if she is not wanted by even one person in the house, and it can make the living conditions unbearable for you and for her. Also, determine whether you will you be the only one taking care of her, or if others will have to pitch in. It is important that everyone understands their responsibilities to the cat.

Can You Afford a Cat?

If you adopted a cat from a shelter or purchased a cat or kitten, you may have spent $75 or you may have spent $750. But that is just the beginning. You need to consider the costs involved in taking take care of your kitty. Not only will the cat need food, litter, scratching posts, toys, and other equipment, but there are visits to the vet, vaccinations, identifications and licenses, and, if you travel, the services of a good cattery. It is also wise to consider pet health insurance—this may seem like an extravagance, but it will save you money in the long run if an unexpected illness or surgery crops up. Be sure that you are financially able to support her. She will repay you a thousandfold.

Do You Have Space For a Cat?

A cat doesn't need a big backyard or acres of space for exercise or sleeping or eating—they feel safer and more comfortable living indoors and can be happy in an apartment, a condominium, or a castle. But there are some space requirements that are very important.

First and foremost is the litter box. Cats need a bit of privacy, so be sure you have a secluded, quiet corner to put the box. Litter boxes should also not be in the same space with their food and water. The odor becomes an issue very quickly for a cat. If the litter box is in the same room with the cat's food, put the litter box on the floor and the cat's food on a shelf or table.

Windows are important for cats; multiple windows are like channels on a TV. Your cat will move from window to window if there is a comfortable place to sit or sleep. Cats fall asleep in front of their televisions just like humans do.

Remember that cats are companions, and they want to be where you are. If, however, you do not want the cat sleeping on your bed or on the furniture, it is important to make sure you have a designated sleeping space for them, and that it established as soon as you bring them home.

A Cat's-Eye View

DEAR CLYDE,
My two-year-old Ragdoll Molly has been scratching and pawing outside of her litter box when she is done using it. Why is she doing that?

You know when you go to the beach and you get sand between your toes? It's annoying, right? Well, it's the same for us with the litter! If Molly scratches every single time she gets out of the box, then she's probably just getting the litter out from between her toes.

Now, if she doesn't scratch every time, then when she does it she is trying to tell you that she's ticked off about the condition of her litter box—maybe it's not clean (would you use the toilet and not flush it every time? I don't think so!), or maybe you changed the brand of litter and she hates it.

So, to help Molly you can do a couple of things. Get a special mat that looks like plastic grass; this helps clean her paws. And keep her litter box clean—and go back to her old litter!

If you want your cat to have some outdoor experience, it is best to build a covered pen or keep the cat on a leash. If you allow your cat to run loose outdoors, you are inviting all types of trouble. While she might never run into the street or chase a motorcycle, if she sees animal activity, her hunting instinct will engage immediately, and she will go after her prey. The unsupervised outdoors is also the domain of feral cats (cats that are not domesticated) which are a serious threat to your cat's health and welfare. Your cat is safer and less likely to get into trouble if you let her watch the world from her favorite window.

Choosing the Purrrfect Feline

You have decided that you need more information about cats. You know there are a lot of differences that make it essential for you to consider all kinds of options. But you have fallen under the special spell of the feline, so look out!

Before picking out your companion, there are a lot of questions to consider—do you want an adult or kitten, male or female, purebred or mixed breed, and so on. All cats are adorable, so answering these questions can help narrow down the field.

Kitten or Adult?

Choosing between a kitten and an adult is hard. We like kittens because they are cute, they offer terrific entertainment, and usually have learned the basics of behavior before they leave the litter. Having a crush on those adorable little balls of fur is not unusual, but it is important to remember that kittenhood, just like childhood, is a very short period. How will you feel about the cat when it becomes an adult? Lavishing attention on a kitten without any limits will achieve the same results it does with children; they will become spoiled and out of control. Kittens are also vulnerable to disease and injury, and their curiosity factor can easily put them into dangerous circumstances, so they need constant supervision and protection.

Because an adult cat is more settled it can be a great addition for an older home, but an adult will have some habits and behaviors that you do not know about, so there will be some adventures. An adult cat can be less rambunctious, but do not let their age fool you. A catnip mouse, a

paper bag, or just a leaf blowing in the wind can release the kitten in the cat. A young adult will show you all its tricks while an older adult may need some inspiration.

Purebred or Mixed Breed?

Purebred cats are a very small percentage of the total cat population—it is estimated that less than 6% of pet cats are pedigreed. The main reason for this is the cost of a purebred kitten. A neutered Maine Coon kitten may cost as little as $550, while a breeding female can cost from $900 to $1500. Prices vary drastically depending upon the breed and its popularity. So, why do people want purebreds?

One of the upsides of having a purebred cat is that you are assured of certain characteristics that are inherent in each breed. For instance, the Siamese is very intelligent, has a very verbal attitude, and is a climber, while the Persian, identifiable by its long, dense fur and its squashed face, is known for being a couch potato.

However, sometimes this upside can also be a downside. Persians have been bred to have the distinctive flat face, but because of this, some Persians develop serious breathing problems. While not all breeds have problems, it is smart to investigate the particular issues that may be inherent in your choice of a purebred.

The best way to determine if a purebred is for you is to do your research. Do not just read about a cat, attend a cat show, talk to breeders, and spend time with the animals. Get acquainted with as many cats as you can. They will help you make a choice.

If you are looking for a purebred but want an adult instead of a kitten, look into breed-specific rescue groups. A sad fact is that people will sometimes abandon these cats for any number of reasons. The purebred rescue group wants to protect the breed and also protect the cats with unique characteristics.

Male or Female?

Males are generally larger than the females in the same litter. They are the clowns and dazzlers, and usually prefer playing and fighting with their litter mates. Entertaining to watch and fun to have around, they frequently maintain kitten-like behavior well into their adult years.

The female, on the other, hand loves attention. She does play but she is interested in establishing her place. She loves petting, being groomed, sitting on laps, and cuddling.

Various behaviors will appear if a cat has not been neutered or spayed. An unneutered male can be very vocal and aggressive and will spray urine to mark his territory. An unspayed female will squirm around with her behind in the air and howl uncontrollably when she goes into heat. The noise can be deafening, and will drive everyone within earshot completely bonkers!

For these reasons and so many more, it is very important to have your cat spayed or neutered. Not only will it save you the frustration of these behaviors, but your cat will be much healthier because of it. An unspayed female can develop problems such as uterine infections and mammary tumors, and males are much more susceptible to prostate cancer and bladder problems. Not getting your cat fixed early on can run into major veterinarian bills down the road.

Longhair or Shorthair?

They each are beautiful in their own way: sleek and shiny short hairs or fluffy and silky longhairs. Time is a big factor in deciding which way to go. Long-haired cats such as Persians and Himalayans must be groomed daily, otherwise their coat will become matted and get out of control in a very short time, and the matts will have to be cut out. Even when a longhair is very good at self-grooming it is impossible for them to keep their coat detangled. A

daily grooming can take anywhere from 15 to 30 minutes, and, even though they may live indoors, long-haired cats need periodic baths. Also, ingesting hair is more likely with a long hair cat, which can lead to hairballs and time spent cleaning them up or giving the cat medication to lessen the occurrence.

There are some longhair cats that do not suffer from matting because of the texture of the hair. The Ragdoll is a good example. The medium-long coat does not mat and has a soft texture like rabbit fur. The tail is bushy and she has a ruff around her neck and longer hair on the hindquarters.

The shorthair cat requires less grooming—once a week is usually enough. There are very distinctive shorthairs such as the American Shorthair and the Siamese, and there are even some hairless varieties (though they are not truly hairless—they have a very light, soft fuzz). The Sphynx is one of them. The Sphynx sweats because of her lack of hair so rather than brushing she requires sponging to keep her clean.

One issue that may be a determinant in your decision is the climate in which you live. A Sphynx will not do well in a perpetually cool climate because her genes have determined she will be hairless. The Maine Coon cat will have long hair wherever she lives, but she will not be nearly as comfortable in the tropics as she is in New England.

There are some mixed breeds that can have long or short hair. The mixture may keep us in suspense until the kitten becomes an adult. Normally a cat develops some fur characteristic by three months and you will then be able to determine whether she will be long or short haired. It is not unusual in a mixed breed litter to find kittens with both long hair and short hair.

Finding the Right Feline

Finding the purrfect cat, even when you have narrowed the choices, will be time consuming. If you have decided on a specific breed then try the local rescue group. If the cat is very rare and you have your heart set on it, research and contact a breeder. The Internet can be your friend in doing this research. The Cat Fanciers Association has a link for breeder referrals and for breed rescue groups. Breeders and rescue groups do want you and the cat to have a loving relationship. They have contracts and warranties so that you can undo what you did, if it turns out to be less than purrfect.

On the other hand, if you are looking for a buddy and the breed is not an issue, there are municipal shelters, pet shelters, and adoption groups in nearly every city. The municipal shelter supported by taxes and fees will only hold stray or unwanted animals for a limited time, because of the cost. They will return animals to owners when they can. However, after a mandated length of time, the pet may be euthanized.

The Society for Prevention of Cruelty to Animals (SPCA) and the Humane Society of the United States (HSUS) operate chapters throughout the country. These organizations take in kittens and adult cats and rescue strays.

Generally they take care of the animals until the owner is found or the animal is adopted into a new home. They take quality care of their cats and kittens and will not let them be adopted until they have had a complete checkup and are in good physical condition. The pet you adopt will be spayed or neutered before it is released to a new home. They are largely volunteer operations maintained by donated hours and dollars.

When you go to these organizations, be aware that they have specific requirements, a fee, and very often a contract that you must sign. They may interview you in depth. There are some that will visit your home before they release the cat. Many of the volunteers have acted as loving foster homes for pets, and they have a vested interest in the cat you want. They will ask about your household, other pets, and if there are small children. Shelters want you to have the right cat, and want to make sure the cat is going to a good home, so this should not be seen as a setback.

There are many kittens and cats needing a home. Selecting the right one will be hard. Most shelters have quiet get-acquainted rooms where you can sit down with a potential buddy and see how well you match. Some kittens will want to play while others will want to be held. A bigger cat might nip or refuse to be held. The animal that re-

sponds to you and communicates its trust is most likely the candidate you will select. Take your time; this relationship is for good.

A Cat's-Eye View

DEAR CLYDE,
My cat Chester is constantly butting me
with his head and rubbing his face all over me!
Is he marking me as his territory?

*Yes, he sure is. We have scent glands all over the
place—on our cheeks, along our tail, on our chin,
and even between our toes, and we love to mark
things as our own. But he's not only marking you,
he's picking up your scent, too.*

*As for the head butts, that's just our way of
showing that we love you—same thing when we
wind ourselves between your legs.*

DEAR CLYDE,
Our Ella is always bringing us animals that
she has killed. Birds, chipmunks—she even left
a dead rabbit next to the Christmas tree!
Is she just showing off?

No, Ella is actually showing you how much she loves
you. She is just trying to reciprocate for all of the
food and love you give her, by bringing home some
fresh food for you! This is a very generous act by
Ella, so make sure that you thank her and then,
when she leaves the room, you can dispose of the
little treasure.

CHAPTER 4

- ♣ **THE** Essentials
- ♣ **CATPROOFING** Your Home
- ♣ **THE** Ride Home
- ♣ **A ROOM** of Her Own

Setting Up House and Bringing Home Your Feline

So you have decided to live together. Now the question is, will the cat or kitten go along with your decision. The adult cat already has expectations based on her prior experiences. The kitten's experience has been limited to her mother and her litter mates. Being new at understanding the cat's mind means you will be doing some guessing. Pay attention to her voice, her expression, and her behavior.

But before you bring the cat to her new home, you will need to get your house ready for her arrival.

The Essentials

If you have not been in a pet store recently, it will be an overwhelming experience. There are endless aisles of toys, food, litter, grooming equipment, and furniture. It is best to just start with the essentials; then once she settles in, you can go back to the pet store for a "shop till you drop" tour.

The Essential Shopping List:

If you are bringing home a kitten, the litter box sides need to be relatively low—two or three inches. If the sides are too high, she will have to use the floor. Covered litter boxes are a matter of preference. Although cats need their privacy, some cats will not use them because they hold in odors. Whether you use an open or a closed box, it will be your job to keep it clean and keep the odor to a minimum. Bleach is an excellent choice for cleaning a cat box. It kills bacteria and is one of the few cleaners that a cat can tolerate.

There are several types of litter available—gravel, clumping, and organic, to name a few. Gravel is the most inexpensive, but clumping is easier to clean. Pellet litter is generally made from recyclable materials. The environmentalists support that use but others say that it is not good for cats. Do not substitute newspaper or beach sand for litter. The ink on the newspaper is harmful, and beach sand has many types of trash and fleas. If you can, find out what the cat has been using and take a few tablespoons of litter that the cat has already used to put into the new box.

Look for bowls that are fairly flat (so they cannot be tipped over) and made of a non-absorbent material such as stainless steel, glass, or porcelain. Be sure you wash them daily.

FOOD

When choosing food for your cat, it is wise to avoid the generic and store brands. Branded foods are the result of veterinary research and are much better for your cat. Also be sure to purchase the proper kind of food—just as there is baby food for humans, there is kitten food for young cats. There are foods for hairball control, for older cats, for cats with gum problems, and of course, for cats with a weight problem. If you do not know what the cat or kitten was eating before you brought her to your home, try small quantities of different kinds to see what she likes best. For more in-depth information regarding specific types of food, see pages 71-75. Never feed cats dog food; they have different needs.

SCRATCHING POST

A scratching post is a must for a cat—it helps pulls the husks from the cat's claws and offers an outlet for some aggressive attitudes. You can purchase many different types of posts in the pet store or make your own. Sisal, a rough rope made of agave or hemp made from a member of the mulberry family are excellent coverings for a scratching posts. Because a cat's scratching behavior is so vigorous, it is important to make something the cat cannot pull over, and it should be high enough that the cat has the opportunity to stretch out full length as she scratches. A support post in your stairwell banister, or any type of interior railing post would make excellent scratchers. When the rope is worn, just peel it off and replace it.

TOYS

Toys that entertain and exercise your cat are important. But just as new parents are inclined to over-indulge a baby, cat staff frequently are guilty of over-buying for a new pet. Restrain from this impulse. You may actually have some ready-made toys and not know it. A ping pong ball is light and responsive, and hard for a kitten to ignore. A slender dowel with an elastic string suspending some feathers and ribbon is a great substitute for a bird. Kittens and adult cats have a hunting instinct; stalking and pouncing are natural activities for felines of all ages. Cats and kittens have powerful jaws and sharp teeth, so be sure to remove any small decorations on the toy so they do not swallow them. Toys with strings should be put away when you are not using them.

CARRIER

Whether soft-sided or hard plastic, make sure you get a carrier that will fit the cat when it is full grown. The cat should have enough room to comfortably turn around. Carriers with a top opening are easiest for getting the cat in and out of the carrier. Carriers that open from the top as well as the side make it easy to put your cat in the bag without a wrestling match.

BED

Cat beds are cute and come in all shapes and sizes but they are not an absolute necessity. Cats sleep in a variety of places and can be fickle at bedtime; many cats will never sleep in a cat bed. Kittens will climb into

the top of a tissue box or settle on freshly washed towels. Cats find the sink is cool on a warm day and a down quilt is purrfect on a cold morning. If you find a cat bed that you just have to have, buy it, but do not be disappointed if she does not sleep in it.

Catproofing Your Home

Before you bring home your feline, it is important to cat-proof the house. There are many things that you as a good owner need to consider. If you see the world as your cat does, it will be easier to see what may cause harm.

Sit down in your kitchen and look around. Why the kitchen? Because it is your cat's favorite room! What does she see? Think like her. Cords on the appliances look like the perfect thing to chew or play with. Decorative plates and pottery on the shelf above the cupboards are a climbing challenge—it may take time, but they can get up there (or fall in the attempt). The cupboard under the sink has a lot of interesting stuff to a cat—can she get in it when you're not around? Once you pinpoint the danger areas you can begin to safeguard them, by putting guards on the cupboards and so forth.

Now, check the rest of the house. It is hard for humans to see some of the hazards that exist, particularly at a cat's and kitten's level. Some potential danger items:

- CORDS for shades and drapes

- SPACES under, behind, or around the refrigerator, the dishwasher, and the fireplace

- PLANTS that may be poisonous

- WASHERS and dryers with the doors left open

- ELECTRICAL cords (including electric blankets)

- PAPER shredder

- SEWING machine and accessories

- LOOSE office supplies (rubber bands, paper clips, etc.)

- RIBBONS and tinsel

- OPEN windows without screens

- CLEANING products

- WASTEBASKETS and garbage cans

Once you identify these danger zones, you can catproof them. Store items in boxes with catproof lids or behind doors that cats cannot open. Be sure that windows without screens are closed, and check screened windows for holes in the screen or loose corners. The screening material needs to be attached firmly to the frame in the event your cat leans or falls against it. If you have a balcony, do not allow the cat to wander there. Birds, insects, or a sudden startling noise are all reasons for a cat to leap or fall without warning. Frequently cats fall asleep on a window sill or narrow ledge, and then fall. The legend that cats always land on their feet is not true, but do not let your new roomie prove it. Falling, particularly for kittens, can do serious harm.

Plants are especially enticing to cats, as they enjoy chewing on them. Check the list on page 176 to see which are poisonous. In order to steer them away from your favorite plant, keep a small container of alfalfa or catnip for her enjoyment. Cats develop a taste for certain human foods despite the fact they are carnivorous; mushrooms, olives, lettuce, spinach, plus the petals of roses are frequently stolen when humans are not paying attention. Be sure that your vet is aware of unusual eating habits your cat develops; some items are okay while others may be harmful.

If you have an attached garage with cat access, be very careful. The warm engine under the hood is a perfect a kitty heater. She may crawl inside or sleep on top of a wheel under the fender. Before you start the engine, give the tires a kick, thump on the hood, and honk the horn. One toxic item that has killed cats and dogs over the years is antifreeze. It has a sweet taste that attracts them. The newer, safe formulation has pylene glycol rather than the toxic ethylene glycol.

Most cats are not eager to ride in the car. There are times, however, when you have to take her to the vet or cattery. Do not leave her alone in the car, even for a few minutes. The interior of the car warms up rapidly and can reach over 100 degrees, even when the outside temperature is cold. Your cat may not survive.

Every year we hear of young children who die because they are left unattended in a locked car. When a pet dies, it does not usually make the news, but it is also horrible.

A Cat's-Eye View

DEAR CLYDE,
Help! I'm exhausted! Every night Maddie plays circus. She waits until I go to bed and then starts running around, meowing, and jumping up on the bed and pawing at me. I've got to get some sleep! What can I do?

Well, first of all, you have to keep in mind that we are nocturnal—it's been bred in us since day one. But also, when you're at work all day we're sleeping, so by the time you get home our day is just starting! (By the way, it's just a myth that we can see in the dark—we just see better than humans do in darker light.) The most important thing is that you don't punish her for her night crazies—she can't help it. But you can make your life a little easier. Try to get her more on your schedule. Instead of letting her veg out with you while you watch the news, keep her awake and tucker her out with some vigorous play time.

The Ride Home

Transporting the cat or kitten to your digs will be your first test: can you make your new roommate feel secure?

Most shelters or rescue centers will provide a cardboard carrier for your new pet, but they are flimsy, so it is best to bring her home in the carrier you have purchased. Do not borrow a bag or carrier from a well meaning friend. Your new cat's sensitive nose will pick up other odors which will only serve to confuse your new roomie. Place a soft, clean towel in the bag, making sure your scent is on the towel.

With a kitten, if she is calm enough, you can carry her home in your lap. A soft hand towel on your lap makes great cuddle material and warmth for your small friend.

Have someone else drive and caution them about honking horns and loud stereo. Pet the kitten and talk in a soft voice to reassure it. Soft mewing is normal in your kitten's world; kittens have only talked to mom so they need to learn your voice. After an initial tenseness, kittens will relax if you make them feel safe. Remember that everything is new; loud noises or sudden moves are to be avoided.

A Room of Her Own

Rather than dumping the new resident out as soon as you close the front door, take her to her room, close the door and sit down to get acquainted. Open the door to her carrier and let her come out on her own—do not try to yank her out before she's ready. If you have a small apartment, put the carrier in a quiet corner and leave it out for her. She needs to have a place of her own that is quiet and out of traffic. Let your new kitten or cat inspect the food area and sample the cuisine. Be sure that fresh water is also available. Do not worry if your kitten or adult cat does not eat right away. They are busy investigating many new stimuli.

The next item is the litter box. Kittens are generally trained by their mothers in the proper use of the box. Adult cats, particularly those who have resided in a shelter or cattery for awhile, know how to use a litter box, but may make a huge display of inspecting the contents. The litter box experience may be your first introduction to your cat's personality. If the box is in a very secluded place the cat may have trouble finding it. Show them where the litter box is by gently placing them in it.

It is important not to place the litter box and food in the same area, as the odors from the litter box will turn them away from the food. With an adult cat, put the litter box on the floor, preferably in a corner (privacy you know), and put the food in an elevated location in another part of the room. With a kitten, create separate areas at floor level until the kitten is capable of jumping easily to another level.

Understanding Cat Behavior

What To Expect

As a cat staffer, you are constantly being evaluated by your feline for job performance. Of course, you must recognize that some cats are not nearly as demanding as others. Cats expect your attention during their waking hours. Fortunately they sleep at least sixteen hours a day. Many, however, choose the remaining eight hours to be those in which you ordinarily sleep. It is one of those habits that you can hope to modify as your relationship develops.

The socializing process for a kitten began with its mother and continues with you. Unless you picked up an unweaned foundling, your kitten will know how to eat from a dish and how to use the litter box. But you and your cat need to bond. Those first few days are important and you will find that the expectations of your cat are very definite.

Eating

Cats can be infuriating for you if you do not understand what they communicate about food, especially at mealtime. It is great fun to have your eighteen-pound Maine Coon doing figure eights around your knees when you are trying to get your old can opener to cut into the lid of her cat food. It is still mildly amusing when she jumps up on the counter and saunters over to supervise your progress. It is not funny when she puts her paw on the can and pushes it away from you. Why does she do that? Because you are taking too long.

She also notices that there is fresh food in plain sight that smells like Coho Salmon. She knows that you love her, so she thinks that you intended for her to have the salmon, not the food in the can. Right in front of your very eyes she helps herself to the salmon and drags it off the counter to take it to her favorite spot. In a very loud voice, you very firmly say, "NO!" She looks at you, startled by your outburst, and politely sits down to wait for further commentary. This is the time to act quickly. Grab the salmon, wrap it in foil, and stick it in the oven where she cannot get to it. Proceed with the can opener. Cats do like to tease their staff.

Your choice of food, and how your cat accepts it, is important. Timing of feeding will be determined by the cat and then you will see if you can modify it to fit your schedule. In the early stages her voice will communicate her feelings. But watch closely and you will soon discover that particular wave of the tail or understand why she sits with her back to you.

Some cats graze all day and you will need to leave dry food for them to eat whenever they feel the need. If your new charge wants to take full advantage of your absence every day, one meal in the morning or evening for an adult will probably allow her to get plenty of sleep while you are out. It is assumed that cats know when they overeat, and dogs do not. Unfortunately cats appear to have picked up some behaviors from dogs or over-attentive owners. Cats will overeat and become very obese. As staff, you need to watch your cat's eating habits and make sure she does not gain too much weight.

Kittens will put you to the test by eating huge quantities and occasionally looking like stuffed toys. You need to follow the recommended quantity guidelines on the kitten's food package or discuss with your vet what is the appropriate quantity for your kitten. The advantage with a kitten just like a child is that they are active and generally burn off the fat they consume rather than store it. Your job as staff is to keep the balance between adequate food, adequate exercise, and keeping your kitten fit and happy.

Do not be surprised if your cat chooses to drink water from other locations: the sink, the toilet, the bathtub, the flower arrangement, and the potted plants. Water from the flowers or used on plants may be contaminated, so remove the temptation. Ordinary tap water is just fine for kittens and cats. If you keep a glass of water on a bedside table, you may find the cat has mastered the art of dipping her paw into the glass and licking it. Remember that she also uses that paw in the litter box, so try to keep your water glass covered.

Playing

Your kitten's needs will include proper playing and facilitating proper scratching. Play time is important, but even more important is how you play.

Your kitten will grab anything that moves quickly through her field of vision. Sometimes staff makes the mistake of letting the kitten choose fingers, toes, and ears as toys. When helping your kitten to learn how to play, never let her think that body parts are toys. Chasing a ping pong ball or a feathered toy on a string is learning how to play and satisfy the hunting instincts. If the toy is mauled the kitten has learned to play. If instead you permit your fingers to be mauled, you have not communicated properly with your kitten. You have established a precedent that will need correction. If you do not correct the behavior, as an adult the cat will have gone from tiny aggressor to heavyweight combatant who can inflict major damage.

At an early age cats will suddenly discover catnip. Catnip (nepeta cataria—a member of the mint family) does work as a stimulant for a cat. However, you might find the catnip mouse from the pet shop is totally ignored. Just as spices and herbs that stay on the shelf too long lose their flavoring capacity, so does the catnip. Catnip will stay fresh if you refrigerate it. Many pet stores carry toys that you can fill with catnip, but putting a handful in the toe of an old nylon will also work just as well. If your cat suddenly loses interest in her toy, refill it with fresh catnip and the play cycle will begin again.

Biting, Nibbling, Attacking

If you bring an adult cat home that demonstrates aggressive habits, immediately use toys and other objects to adjust behavior. If the new cat insists on attacking you, respond immediately by clapping your hands and a definitive "no;" getting mad at the cat or swatting a cat is simply returning like behavior. You need to change the cycle of behavior. Retaliation does not work.

If cat communication is new, you will need to learn the difference between aggressive biting and love nibbles. One of the ways that a cat will express affection is a gentle nibble or head butt. The adult cat learned these displays from her mother. If the nibble becomes a bite then say "no" to the behavior. Normally, love nibbles are a means of communicating that whatever the behavior is—grooming, scratching the head, stroking the jaw—she approves.

Scratching

Scratching is normal cat behavior. The fact that a cat can shred your upholstery implies that you need to take steps to prevent this from happening. Sometimes you need more than one place or one type of scratching post to make sure your cat does not destroy your house. An adult cat

A Cat's-Eye View

Clyde the cat answers your questions about

ODD BEHAVIOR

DEAR CLYDE,
It never fails, Figaro can spot the person in the room who doesn't like cats, and he immediately goes to them. Can't he see that they don't want him around?

There's a completely logical explanation for that. You see, when we meet other cats, they will try to stare us down, in order to take over our place. So when all of these people come into Figaro's space and stare at him and try to pick him up (which he sees as showing their power over him), he doesn't want to have anything to do with him.

Now, imagine Figaro seeing a person who is not staring at him, and who is actually paying him no attention at all. Well, that person must not want to take over Figaro's space, so he immediately thinks that person is going to be friendly, and off he goes to try and jump in that person's lap!

Makes perfect sense, doesn't it!

may need to be encouraged to scratch; rubbing the post with catnip is a good way to get her attention. Kittens take a while before they are responsive to catnip.

Sleeping

Many new owners will have a cat fit about where to put the cat bed. Stop right now! Cats sleep wherever they are when they get sleepy. Even cats in a crate will sleep in the litter box rather than on the nice clean towel provided as a bed. Cats make their own decisions and because sleeping occupies so much of their time, they are not about to let you tell them where they are going to sleep. If there is an electric blanket or a down comforter on your bed, on a very cold night, the cat will sleep there. If it is a hot summer night, the cat will likely sleep on her back in front of the air conditioner. If the cat has stayed up to watch a little TV, she may decide to sleep on the window ledge, just in case.

Cat sleep patterns are varied. The phrase cat-nap is clearly accurate. This is a quick, light sleep with eyes just barely closed until something interesting happens. If your cat has all four paws tucked underneath her and her eyes closed, this could be a cat-nap. Like a drag racing car, she can accelerate from nap to leap in a nanosecond. There is

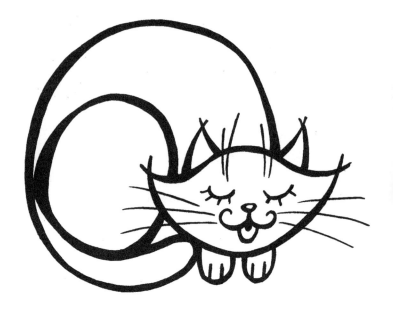

a longer light sleep where the cat settles down to sleep in a selected spot and may stay put for as much as a half hour. This light sleep may lead to a deep sleep cycle that is usually distinguished by the cat making noises and twitching. The cat may return to the light sleep mode after a few minutes of deep sleep. This two-cycle sleep pattern can last for several hours. When you discover your cat asleep on its back with all four legs extended in a relaxed position, you can be sure that your cat feels secure.

What's Hers is Hers, and What's Yours is Hers

It is wise to start with the assumption that everything you have is hers. If you are not used to sharing, the cat will make her demands very clear from the outset.

Once your cat or kitten has adjusted to her surroundings, usually a week is plenty for an adult and a bit longer for a kitten, she will test her environment. Not unlike Goldilocks, she will want to taste your food, sit in your chair, and sleep in your bed. She will tell you that you are being very selfish if you insist she eat her own food, sit in another chair, or move her from your bed so you can get into it.

If you train her to not jump on the kitchen counter or the dining room table, you can be assured that she will do so while you are out. She needs to know her whole environment, so do not be surprised by paw prints found in a forbidden place. However, do not scold her after the fact; she has no idea what you're talking about, it is old news.

All the chairs that get sunshine, are beneath windows, are in front of the computer, or you having chosen to sit in, are hers. She obviously will not use them all at the same time, but you can be sure that once you are comfortably settled in a chair, it will suddenly be her chair. She may tell you to move or, failing that, simply jump onto your lap. If you are sitting in the chair with a book or knitting, she will do something useful to assist you, turning pages, biting knitting needles, or unwinding the ball of yarn. Choosing to get up is no longer an option.

Litter Box or Toilet Training

Since we are considering where your cat lives, and how to make her life pleasant, there is an option to the litter box you might want to consider: your cat may be toilet trained. It sounds outlandish, but it is doable. There are some caveats to consider if you want to try this approach. It is easier for the cat if she does not have to share a bathroom. Remembering to put the seat down and leave the lid up is essential to the cat being able to use a toilet. The behavior modification process takes about three weeks, and it is important to encourage the cat's behavior. The odor-free environment of using a toilet is quite satisfying to a cat. There are a couple of excellent books complete with pictures that explain the process. Two of the books are listed in the reference bibliography.

CATisthenics and Feline Fitness

CHAPTER 6

Have you heard the remark, "Pet owners look like their pets"? What a wonderful thing to think that we look like our intelligent, agile, sleek feline. The issue is, how do we care for a kitten or adult cat to keep them fit? Fitness is dependent on several things. The first is diet.

It is important to understand that cats have different nutritional needs from their humans. In the world where cats are left alone, live outside, or have to fend for themselves, they do eat human food—table scraps, leftovers, even garbage. That does not mean that they like it or that it is good for them; it means they are hungry. We picky humans would eat whatever we could find in the same circumstances. Hunger is a universal experience, and we deal with it in a like manner.

The Stages of Feeding

The kitten stage

If your new feline is a recently weaned kitten, the eating experience is still quite new. Mother cats are usually very good about introducing their offspring to food and weaning them at the same time. The mother demonstrates that the squishy stuff in the bowl has a fine aroma, an excellent texture, and tastes good. It fills tiny stomachs rapidly satisfying hunger. Kittens make the connection quickly. Usually the kitten has made the complete transition to her new food by eight weeks.

Kittens, like kids, love to extend the eating experience by playing with their food. Occasionally you will find a kitten sitting in the food dish. The dish was so big that climbing into it seemed to be the only option. It is not wise to scold a kitten sitting in the midst of her food—just find a smaller dish and put some food in it from the big dish. The kitten might go on her own to the small dish, or you may have to lift her out of the big dish. As long as the kitten is reunited with the food, life will be beautiful.

The adult stage

Your kitten will grow rapidly during her first six to eight months. She will go through the gangly stage as she grows into her ears and long legs. She will entertain you and become more demonstrative as she grows. The kitten diet will be appropriate until she is a year old. When the kitten becomes a young adult, the diet will change.

This time for a feline is comparable to being a teenager. It will also be the first time that your juvenile will really test you. Whenever there is a transition or change in environment you must be careful. Cats love and depend upon "routine" as the structure of their existence. Surprises are something they give to you, but do not particularly enjoy for themselves. Changing the diet from kitten food to adult food needs to be managed very carefully. The first week of transition, incorporate one quarter cup of the new food with each three-quarters cup of kitten food. The second week, give her equal parts of kitten food and adult food. The third week, give your kitten three-quarters cup of adult food and only one-quarter cup of kitten food. The following week try just adult food.

If your cat is reluctant to change take more time to introduce the new food. Start with smaller changes and let them stay at a given level longer. If your kitten has had only canned food, try an additional small bowl with dry

food. A very human approach that some cats are quick to grasp is the "clean plate club." If they eat the new food in the bowl, they are rewarded with a treat, more food. The danger in this approach is that your cat might eat more than she really needs.

Feline Nutrition

Unfortunately, your cat is not going to explain her nutritional needs to you. She expects you to make those decisions. After all, you are staff and it is your job. You knew some things about cats before bringing one home. You knew that lions, tigers, cougars, and, by extrapolation, house cats were carnivores. Being a carnivore means meat-eating and that isn't very specific. For cats there are some specific needs and some non-essentials.

The non-essentials

We know for a fact that two foods that many humans love are chocolate and onions (though usually not in the same dish!). Neither of these foods should ever be fed to cats. Chocolate is toxic and onions can lead to anemia in cats. But neither item is made from meat so we hope the opportunity never arises for your kitten or cat to sample them. Not so obvious is the idea of meat that is raw being a danger to kittens or cats. Raw meat, poultry, and fish are appealing to cats because they recognize the odor instinctively. The problem is that raw animal products can carry parasites which can lead to all kinds of sickness, including worms. Cooking will eliminate the risk. Your cat might not be sure of your ability in this department; just the same, pretend you are a competent cook. Keep the cooking simple and fast. If you use the microwave, be sure the food cools sufficiently before giving it to her.

There are foods that some cats will decide they need. Cats have been known to eat cantaloupe, avocados, asparagus, mushrooms and olives. If your cat gets into something unusual, it is a good idea to check with the vet.

The essentials

A cat's diet is protein and fat. There are several important vitamins and minerals. The diet should include manganese, zinc, copper and Vitamins A, B and E. Fatty acids are important to skin and fur condition and fiber is important to the digestion. Taurine, an amino acid, is essential to your cat's well-being found in meat, poultry, and fish and in animal by-products. A diet without adequate taurine may lead to blindness in kittens and heart problems in adults. Branded cat foods will show the ingredients on the can or bag. You may want to feed your cat small amounts of canned food two or even three times per day rather than one large serving. The total amount per day should follow the package guidelines so you do not over feed her. Feed your pet at established times and then remove the dish.

A well-balanced cat diet comes in three forms:

MOIST (CANNED)

Canned food comes in dozens of flavors and textures, including ground, sliced, and shredded. On the upside, canned cat food contains up to 70% water, so it is a good source of liquid for your cat, and it is by far the most palatable. On the downside, it can be expensive and has more of an odor than dry food. If you feed your pet the canned food, do not leave it out as it will go bad; opened cans need to be refrigerated.

SEMI MOIST

Semi-moist food has the appearance of dry food, but the bits are soft. Many of the special treats are prepared as moist food. This is handy food to have on hand, as the container or pouch is resealable and doesn't need refrigeration. However, semi-moist food tends to have more sugar than moist or dry food, which can lead to obesity and health problems.

Dry food has the definite advantage of being the most economical and convenient. It does not need refrigeration and can sit out all day. Many cats enjoy grazing; they are not necessarily interested in eating, but are satisfied as long they can see food in the bowl. Dry food offers balanced nutrition, great taste, will not go bad, and helps to prevent plaque by not building up on your cat's teeth.

Wet vs. Dry

The debate about dry food versus wet food is endless. Some say a steady diet of dry food is preferable because it helps keep the cat's teeth clean, while others say that wet food is best because get more water into the cat's diet and the food tastes better. Both sides have valid points, and most staffers prefer to give their cats a mixture of both, keeping dry food out at all times and serving a small portion of wet food once a day. Whatever works for your cat is fine; the most important thing to remember is that the food you feed them must be well balanced.

If your cat discovers an empty dish, expect loud howls or even a nip of your hand to point out the desperate situation she is in. Be very respectful of the sudden concern and put something in the bowl so she cannot see the bottom. Remember that cats have expectations and creating a stressful situation involving food is counter productive. Many owners point out that grazing cats do not seem to have weight problems. Since she knows you faithfully provide food for her, the cat may not feel she must gobble every last morsel.

Cats are happy with routine. You may think that your cat has become bored with her food, because you are bored doing the same thing every day. Actually cats like having the same food. You can give a treat once in a while, a tidbit from your plate—no more than a tablespoon—or a commercial moist treat may be interesting. The diet that is prepared specifically for a cat should not be supplemented. Be prepared for your cat to sniff the bit of food on your plate and reject it; she is curious but not foolish.

Tummy problems

As your cat ages, she may develop problems that are familiar to humans. One of the most common is constipation. Her normal diet is based in protein and fat, and has very little fiber. Her digestive system begins to bog down. If she is not drinking enough water, things really slow down. A simple solution to the problem is cooked pumpkin. Give her one or two teaspoons at mealtime, she will probably lick it from the spoon; cats like the taste. It is not generally available in small quantities so remove it from the can and freeze it in small bits. That way you will be prepared and she will not need to worry.

Why Isn't She Eating?

If a cat stops eating you as staff need to recognize that something in your cat's environment may have caused stress or fear or pain totally unrelated to food. This is your cat communicating a problem with something that is obvious to her but not to you. You need to do a quick assessment to find the source of the problem.

Are bright eyes dull?

Are her gums sensitive?

Is she lethargic?

Does she have diarrhea?

Is she constipated?

Is she vomiting?

If the answer to any of these is "yes" it is best to take her to the veterinarian right away—these symptoms could be indications of a larger problem and, left untended, could result in liver failure or worse.

If you have determined that she is not ill, check for these changes:

♦ DID YOU FORGET to clean or change the litter box?

♦ DID YOU FORGET to wash her bowls or give her fresh water?

♦ DID YOU CHANGE the brand or type of cat food without working up to it? Read how to introduce a kitten to a new diet on page 68.

♦ DID YOU MOVE ANYTHING from its usual location or add something new?

If the cat and the cat's personal items are not the problem, consider stress as a possible cause. Is there a new member in the household, of either the two-legged or four-legged variety? That can be stressful, and we will deal with it in the next chapter. Is there construction, painting, or major cleaning going on? Both sounds and odors are magnified many times compared to what humans experience. Be sure you do not used ammonia-based cleaners around your cat. The odor will drive them off.

The weather could also be the culprit or your kitty may have gotten into some other food and not be hungry. If you suspect it is just a bit of attitude and nothing serious on the behalf of the cat, let it go. Your cat will not starve in a day or two. In fact, fasting may have some benefits.

Slimming Down

Cats have some very human traits. They want to look good on the one paw—watch how thoroughly they groom and how frequently—but on the other paw, they throw caution to the wind when Thanksgiving comes around. Indeed the split personality of a cat is most obvious when your cat is on the counter, eyeing the turkey and grooming at the same time.

Cats are not formatted to be fat. Their instincts are alive and well even in domesticated cats. It is normal for her to run, leap, stalk, and chase as part of her daily routine. Letting her eat too much allows her to be fat and disables her. The normal weight of any given cat depends on many factors. It is not unusual for a Maine Coon male cat to weigh eighteen pounds. But it would be a very overweight Siamese male to weigh that much.

How do you know if your pet is overweight? Pick her up. With a shorthair cat you will feel her ribs immediately under the skin. The longhair cat requires sliding your fingers into the roots of the hair to feel the skin. While you hold the cat gently around the rib cage, you should be able to count her ribs. She has a total of thirteen pairs. If you cannot feel any ribs, the cat is obese. A long haired cat may look like she's overweight because of her fur, or the fur could be hiding a very overweight cat.

There are some general rules about the weight of cats. One is that a female is generally lighter weight than her male counterpart. There can be a two- to four-pound difference between male and female cats of the same breed and age. A neutered male does not require as many calories as a tom cat. It is important to cut down on calories if you have recently had a male neutered. It is not normal that the neutered or spayed cat automatically becomes overweight.

Cats will become couch potatoes if you let them. As staff, you must communicate with your cat about food and the need for exercise.

The Kitty Athletic Club

It was not so long ago that your kitty was chasing ping pong balls, attacking numerous catnip mice, and trying to fly from the top of a lamp to the Christmas tree. What happened to all that energy and athletic prowess? Of course, kitty was a kitten and now she is an adult.

Check with the vet if you think your cat has gained more than ten percent body weight as an adult cat. By human standards we could be thinking in terms of ten to fifteen pounds. A cat normally weighing ten pounds has gained ten percent with just one pound. It might not seem like much but it is a warning. If the vet agrees that the cat is overweight or even on the heavy end of normal, he might suggest a different diet. Likewise, the prescription could be more exercise. Those antics that you enjoyed watching and participating in while she was a kitten are the same activities that are necessary now as exercise.

The trainer at the gym will tell you that exercise is important and that exercise will not do any good unless you exercise regularly. What could be better than a new activity in your kitty's routine? Your cat will be delighted to have a new regular activity that she can look forward to, and this athletic activity should be a daily routine.

Whatever exercise you do, it is important to start slowly if your cat is very overweight. A cat that has done little more than walk to her litter box, walk to her food dish, or sleep in the sun, is out of shape or old or both. Even twenty year old cats will attempt play just to prove to you that you can't retire yet. Keeping her in shape will aid her in having a long, healthy life.

Here are some exercises to try:

THE OLD FAVORITES

Try something she used to enjoy as a kitten. Get her a new ping pong balls, a catnip mouse, or a bouncing feather toy.

TAKE A WALK

Most people think of only walking dogs, but a cat can enjoy a walk, too. It requires that your cat wear a leash and harness, and you may have to stop frequently for some exploring, but he benefit is that both of you get some exercise!

THE LASER-LIGHT DANCE

Using a laser light, try a little teasing that does not require much more than moving the front paws and the head. This might last for just a few minutes, but can be repeated two or three times during the day. As the cat becomes more alert, increase the distance the cat needs to reach. Keep increments coming until the cat is moving her entire body. Watch for the tail to twitch and snap at the end; this is commonly seen when the cat is hunting. It is also an indication that your cat is interested in the quick moving object.

THE ATTACKER

Progress from laser lights to a toy attached to a string
or elastic on the end of a pole. Dangle the toy just off
the floor so that the cat can attack her prey. Allow
her to catch the toy periodically and then substitute a toy she can attack on her own. Be careful with
toys that involve long strings or elastic; put them
away in a closet so the cat cannot play with them
unsupervised.

THE TREASURE HUNT

This activity requires a cat condo. Place a quarter teaspoon of food on several different levels of the condo.
Help her to discover the first treasure, and then encourage more hunting. Keep the tidbits tiny and well
spaced for maximum benefit.

As you progress into a more active mode, vary the toys,
the game and the location. Keep the time of the activity
on a schedule so she is ready to play. A twenty-minute
play period where she interacts with you and spends some
time playing on her own will improve her fitness and her
appearance, but it may take some time for her to work up
to it.

A Cat's-Eye View

Clyde the cat answers your questions about

TOYS

DEAR CLYDE,
I'd like to get my new kitten, Miranda, some toys, but there are so many to choose from! I don't know what he'd like! Any ideas?

We love anything that crinkles—the crinklier the better! They remind us of crickets, bugs, and birds outside, and they're just fun to play with. Here's another great toy that you can make: take some feathers, gather them up with string, and attach it to a wooden stick. Chester will feel like he's chasing a bird! Most importantly, don't let him use your hands as a toy—he'll get used to doing htat, and then all of a sudden you're going to have a grown cat gnawing on your hands!

Once she is comfortable moving about increase the level of activity with her. Leaping and chasing are instinctive activities and she will enjoy doing them. Running up and down hallways or racing up and down stairs in pursuit of flying wads of paper will be easier and more frequent activities requiring little encouragement.

What's That Crazy Cat Doing Now?

As a cat staffer, there is one basic lesson to learn above all else. Your cat is very smart. She will try all types of behavior. Some of it is instinct-driven. A domesticated cat still has instincts despite the sedate cover she tries to hide behind. She will learn your routines in order to take advantage of them. She will wait in the kitchen for you after she wakes up from her late afternoon nap because that is when she knows you prepare food. As soon as you climb out of bed in the morning she has learned to jump under the covers because you left a nice warm spot. She knows those big brown paper bags are how food is transported by humans. She will inspect them personally when you bring them into the house. If she purrs while on your lap, she knows you will probably pet her and let her stay there.

It Comes Naturally

A black streak just flew up the spiral stairs and disappeared down the next landing and there was a loud crash. By the time you get to the bottom of the landing, a calm and composed black cat is carefully grooming her whiskers. A bouquet of red roses is all over the floor along with water, rose petals, and a heavy, unbroken glass vase. She gets up and, avoiding the puddle, walks daintily to the door. With her tail gently curling back and forth at the top, she blinks at you and walks into the next room. She has no clue why you are red-faced, out of breath, and have your hands on your hips.

The black streak is not a playful kitten or a recently acquired feral cat. She is a healthy, ten-year-old, domestic shorthair. This behavior is normal for her after her morning poop. As a kitten, by climbing those nine steps one at a time, and napping at the top before proceeding, she learned that there was more to the world than her room at the bottom of the spiral stairs. Her speed has improved over the years and she can jump from the landing without using the steps.

Curiosity is what drove her to learn to climb those steep stairs. But does she do this daily ritual because she cannot remember what is at the top of the steps, or is it because she feels responsible and needs to verify everything is in place, or could it be that she just loves to race up and down stairs because she feels so good?

The answer is that all three reasons could be right and maybe there are more reasons. She regards the entire home as her domain. She does not like doors to be closed because she has not learned how to open them without calling staff for assistance. So she races up the stairs, checks all the doors, and then marks any item she has not rubbed lately. When staff checks on her, she quietly waves them away letting her tail indicate everything is fine.

Of late, we have discovered that she does not stop as frequently to check things on her way through the rooms. She seems to be working on improving her speed and her leaps. Her speed and her leaps are instinctual behavior as much as her territorial marking. When she has to share the spiral stairs with staff, she waits so they have a head start, and then she bounds up the outer edge of the steps across the floor to the landing and leaps over the three steps from the landing to the floor. If anyone gives chase, she will continue the game sometimes flattening her ears pretending she's an aggressor and then sit down and stare with ears erect.

The blink is another special behavior. Ordinarily she will stare until you respond. But sometimes, if this is her first encounter of the day, she will blink, acknowledging you with her visual "hello." Eyes, ears, tail, whiskers, voice, mouth and whole body all relay information about how she feels at the moment.

What Does It Mean?

Cats are as individual as the humans with whom they live. As you live with your new kitty, she will exhibit behaviors that are exclusive to her. Your job, as cat staff, is to understand what the behaviors mean, what is she telling you.

Cat staff can respond differently depending up how the messages are transmitted. The woman who believes that cats are furry aliens is certain that cats understand every word we say but pretend otherwise. It is just as likely that cats don't communicate directly because they consider communication a great game. Every time we acknowledge their wishes, we get a point. If we miss the same clue every time, then the points are deducted. Anyone who has spent time as cat staff will have a slightly different idea about cat communication.

Eyes

Cat's eyes are fascinating. They can mesmerize or tease or terrify. Frequently neophytes spend hours talking about eye color without ever noticing what the cat is trying to say. Indeed the blue, green, amber, and variegated coloring of the iris is lovely. A big, round-eyed stare is more important. She is staring at you to find out what you are doing. If those eyes begin to narrow, something is afoot! It could be that she is going to wander over and mark your ankle. Or it could be that she has decided to tell you she's hungry and will issue a demanding meow. Of course, she may just start grooming because she has no plan at all or close her eyes for a quick nap.

The changing of the eye shape accompanied with other signals tells you more. Wide open, round (almond shaped) eyes are generally a positive signal. If the eyes stay wide and her tale switches slightly, she may be contemplating mischief. If the eyes begin to narrow and the ears move back, the indication is more negative. Watch out!

Ears

The cat's ears sit atop the head so she can hear sounds from all 360 degrees. She is capable of moving one ear at a time to track sounds. Watch your kitty when there is a conversation. She will flick her ears in the direction of the speakers. Words that might get her serious attention are eat, food, treat and hungry. If she is sleeping or playing, the minute you use a can opener, she will be at your side. She has very sensitive hearing and does not respond positively to loud noises. A sudden loud noise will send her running to the nearest hideaway. The sudden clap of hands coupled with a loud "no" is effective as a training technique because cats have such keen ears.

The positive, satisfied cat usually has ears forward at attention (except for the purebred cats with folded ears). The cat in stalking or hunting mode may be creeping

about on her belly, but the ears are up until the final leap. They seem, sometimes, to rotate like radar. When the ears go down, more negative activity is on the way. An angry, frightened or aggressive cat will flatten her ears against the side of her head. Until you know her signals very well, this is clearly not the time to attempt to pick up the cat.

Whiskers

The lovely, long whiskers on the face of an adult cat are elegant, but the tiny face of a kitten is exaggerated by huge ears and long whiskers, so the kitten appears perpetually startled. Don't worry—she will grow into her equipment.

The whiskers are very important as part of the cat's sensing system. One function of the whiskers is to determine if she can fit through an opening. If she can thrust her head into a hole or behind a door left ajar, she will usually enter it. A contented, happy, and attentive cat will have a stunning array of whiskers fanning out from her face and sometimes slightly forward reaching. But if she is fearful, aggressive, or angry, she will bring her whiskers into her jowls, just as she flattens her ears against her head. Be aware of her careful grooming, and never allow the whiskers, eyebrows, or long stiff hair on the back side of her front legs to be cut or pulled out. She will occasionally lose a whisker, but a new one will grow in given time. Sometimes the color of her whiskers changes with age; black cats frequently have black whiskers which will turn white as they get older.

A Cat's-Eye View

Clyde the cat answers your questions about

BITING

DEAR CLYDE,
My four-year-old cat, Jax, loves to be petted, but sometimes she will all of a sudden turn and bite me! Why does she do that?

Sounds to me like Jax is just telling you she's had enough—yes, it's true, even the most lovey-dovey of us will get fed up with petting! Jax probably gave you a bunch of signals that she wanted you to knock it off—no purring, lashing her tail around, flicking her ears, maybe even growling—and biting was her last resort. If you just watch out for her signals, you can avoid her taking a bite out of you.

Mouth

The mouth is another part of the sensing system The sensing of smells by curling the upper lip is called flehming. This attribute permits the cat to have an extremely accurate sense of smell right from birth. Occasionally, humans mistake the open mouth for panting. They really are just trying to work the aromas in their neighborhood.

Although a cat obviously cannot smile like the Cheshire Cat, she will bare her teeth when she is angry or afraid. Tiny kittens, not yet familiar with humans, will indulge in this behavior. If an adult cat has bared her teeth and is growling and hissing, it is best to leave her alone. She can inflict major damage.

Tail

Everyone who has ever spent time with cats knows that the tail is really the talking part of the cat. Whether it is a huge plume or bony rail, the tail tells the tale.

When she is stalking prey, real or imagined, a cat will stretch her tail out and rapidly twitch it. It is only the moment

when she is ready to leap that the twitching stops. This motion is very different from the casual, happy-go-lucky tail-up wave of the top third or so of her tail that she offers as she strolls from one napping place to another. This attitude means she feels good. The cat whose tail is down and lashing back and forth very deliberately is likely to be growling or hissing as well. This is not stalking; this is aggression and anger.

If a cat is truly fearful she will carry tail down between her legs. She will also exhibit this behavior if she has been frightened by a sudden, loud noise such as thunder or a car backfiring.

As your kitten grows to adulthood, these tail signals will become refined. Combined with vocalizing and body posture, you will begin to differentiate what facts the cat is communicating.

Purrrfect Personalities

There are more than 88 million cats in the USA, according to the Humane Society of the United States. (There are 74 million dogs, in case you need to know the competition.) Although it is not easy to pigeon-hole their personalities, we do refer to cats by labels which seem to have significance.

The "fraidy cat" label is usually applied to cats who hide under the bed, who do not want you to watch them eat, who only use the litter box after you go to bed, or are not welcoming to strangers. This behavior often stems from experiences with rough treatment and loud sounds early in their lives. For example, a kitten that could never eat because food was always stolen or she was never allowed to finish, is tense about eating. If there are people or other pets around she either won't eat or she gobbles her food. A sudden loud noise is doubly frightening for a cat. The issue of surprise goes against the cat's need for things to be orderly, scheduled, or planned. Add to that the enormous sensitivity they have to sound, and it only takes one exposure to terrify a kitten or a cat.

A cat that has had negative experiences or has been mistreated can learn to trust you and family members if you work with her. It is not reasonable to expect her to suddenly be friends with every human who comes along, but she will, with love and attention, become your friend.

The opposite of our "fraidy cat" kitty is the "party girl." She loves to be petted, cuddled, and to play every waking moment. She is a very well socialized cat. This is a wonderful trait for a first time cat household. She seems to respond and communicate without effort. The only concern about this trait is that she is able to get along with whoever comes along. She needs to be a house cat, or she might wander off with just any friendly human. She will probably be bored if she is left alone all day, so make sure you give her lots of attention.

A socialized kitten is very good as household social director, and a truly well-socialized cat can manage several people at a time without anyone feeling slighted. A choice of laps is good, but the cat will be very careful to avoid creating a competition among laps. The cat always appreciates someone who comes bearing gifts or who functions as team mate in a rowdy game of hide-and-go-seek or ping pong ball soccer. This person can always be counted on for a fresh catnip mouse.

Still, a socialized cat has only one true friend. This sometimes stems from a gene possibly inherited in the random mix of traits that originated in the Maine Coon or American Bobtail. Both of these breeds are described as faithful, loyal, loving and easily socialized. It is likely the ideal cat is waiting to choose you rather than you choosing her. She was the kitten that jumped out from under a newspaper to get your attention or an adult cat that reached out and tapped your arm gently. This ideal cat had a competent mother who was attentive to the needs of her litter. She was neither the runt of the litter nor the aggressive boss. She was the kitten that played with her litter mates. She learned early that grooming was a good thing even if a little rough sometimes. Food was important, but since it was always available it was not the most important thing in her life (Mom was probably a grazer). This cat will identify herself to you with interesting behavior, voice, and appearance.

What Happens at Night?

Every morning when you go into the kitchen you sense that someone has been there. Indeed, the paw prints on the counter are an immediate clue. Sometimes there is cat hair in the sink; the cat might have been checking for dirty dishes with a morsel of food left on them, or perhaps she was thirsty and gone in search of water. Cats, just like children, know that kitchen water is better than bathroom water. The door of the refrigerator hides tremendous treasures. The cat tries to open that door every night. She walks across the stove, and checks the burners for pan fallout. Night time is a good time for cats to hunt. They have the kitchen to themselves, the dark makes for easy hiding, and everyone is asleep.

Knowing that the cat likes to prowl at night is a signal to you. Be sure that you put food away and the dishes are in the dishwasher or at least rinsed. Put anything that is dangerous to the cat—cleaners, solvents, sponges—in a drawer or cabinet. Vegetables and plants left on a coun-

ter top are an invitation to taste. If you know the cat is snooping, leave the little tin of green grass or catnip where she can find it. If she is a grazer, make sure that there is a small amount of dried food in her bowl. It is safer for her to find cat food than something unknown.

If your cat finally tires of her midnight marauding, she is likely to take up a new activity. She might decide that sleeping with you in your bed is tempting. Depending upon where you live, she might take up night stalking. Once a cat discovers animal life at night in her house, she won't rest. There was a warm night that moths had gathered around a light. When the light was left on after everyone went to bed, the resident cat hunted moths. Although the staff slept through this event, the evidence was all around them in the morning. The cat had seen fit to share the moths and had covered the bed and pillows with moths and moth wings.

She Does That to Get Attention

If a cat is stressed, she might resort to strange behavior. It seems that all cats have something that pushes their buttons. Finding out what triggered the behavior would save us from lots of retaliatory action. Cats respond on the moment. They do not carry grudges and they do not know what delayed punishment is about. It behooves us to look at immediate but not necessarily related actions.

Imagine a ten-pound cat running at you full tilt and grabbing your calf as she passes. It is painful, bloody, and frightening. Why would she do that? By the time you have stopped the bleeding, the cat is sitting quietly watching you and strolls over to nuzzle your hand. She seems calm and content. Within the week, this happens two more times. The third time, you stomp your foot, clap, and shout "No!" The cat is stunned.

Why did it start? The cat is most likely resorting to the playful behavior she had when she was a kitten. Unfortunately, she has outgrown the kitten body and didn't perceive anything amiss when she launched her ten pounds. Nor was she aware that razor sharp fangs would elicit such a loud response. If you allowed her to bite and nip as a kitten, you could be responsible as the cause of this action.

If indeed the cat thought she was playing, she might have been looking for attention. There are only a few choices for a cat when she wants attention. She can meow, she can mark and nuzzle, she can bump, or she can bite. If your adult cat is suddenly biting when she never has before, you need to watch her carefully.

Notice whether your cat approaches you with everything positive in her demeanor: forward ears, round eyes, tail up waving at the top, whiskers fanned, and mouth closed. If that is not what you see, do not turn your back on the cat, just keep staring. It may not solve the cat's situation, but it is likely the cat will stop, sit down, and stare back.

Kids and Cats

Very young children should not be encouraged to interact with cats or kittens. Until a child is six or seven, it is hard for them to understand what "gentle" means. Even when you think the child is ready, the contact should be supervised. If children are left alone with a cat too early in the relationship, you may not like the results. An adult cat may simply run away and hide. This is instinctual behavior for her. Some children might see this as an invitation to chase her. If they find the cat, and corner her, the cat will react defensively. Her body will tighten, her tail will lash back and forth, and her ears and whiskers will flatten against the sides of her head. She will bare her teeth and growl or hiss. The children need to understand this is not entertainment; this is serious and the cat is ready to defend herself. The cat should be left alone; the children should retreat. Otherwise the cat may attack and do serious damage.

The fearful cat may not work out if there are other pets or young children in the home. Your other pets might sense right away that the new cat is afraid. They may hassle or haze the newcomer, making the situation worse. Children who are used to a certain behavior pattern with the other pets might not be able to understand the need to treat the newcomer differently. This fearful kitty is likely to do better where she will become the sole focus of positive attention and affection.

Kittens and adult cats should never be given as surprise gifts to children. Children need to learn that cats are a responsibility, and unlike a toy, need regular, continuous attentive care.

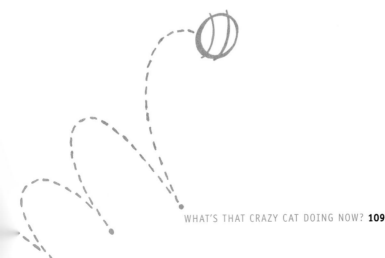

CHAPTER 8

- ✦ DECLAWING and Other Options

- ✦ WHEN is a House Cat an Outside Cat?

- ✦ KITTY Kamp

- ✦ LET'S Hit the Road Together

Some Decisions
Are Hard to Make

Deciding to bring a cat home was an easy decision. But not all decisions in your pet's life will be easy ones.

Declawing and Other Options

Declawing involves removal of the cat's toe bone up to the first knuckle. It is major surgery and can have complications. Without claws she cannot climb, cannot safely jump, and cannot protect herself from other animals. If you need to protect rugs, upholstery, or drapes, there are alternatives to declawing that are not traumatic.

NAIL COVERS

Soft Paws, are acrylic nail covers that cover the claws so that the motion of scratching is not damaging. They are replaced every few months and come in a variety of colors, so you can have matching manicures. Your cat cannot discern color, but she will be very happy if you make your life compatible with hers.

TRAINING

Training a kitten or a cat is a matter of catching them in scratching behavior and taking them to the post and putting their paws on it. A rubbing of fresh or dried catnip will add appeal to the process for an adult cat. When the cat extends her claws and pulls at the covering, praise her. When she finishes give her a small treat. Reward and praise the behavior when it is done in the correct place. Use a vigorous "no" if the scratching occurs in the wrong place and immediately move her to the correct place. During the modification (training) process, protect those places she has attempted to scratch with double sided tape. She will not like the sticky surface.

Clipping your kitty's claws a practice that should begin at an early age, and if it is, regardless of your cat's
size, she will cooperate. The secret is how to hold
her and how much of the claw is clipped. Hold the
cat on your lap with her back against your body. Use
your left hand to hold the paw and with your forearm
against her body, use your right hand to hold the clippers. With the pad side down, put the fingers of your
left hand under the pad and your thumb on top of the
toes. Press gently with your thumb and the claws will
extend. Clip just the opaque curved tip of the claw. If
you clip too much you will cut the quick which hurts,
so be very careful. If you do cut the quick, quickly
apply a stiptic pencil to stop the bleeding. It is better
to cut quickly and take off just the very pointed end
of the claw. If you are quick and the cut is clean, you
can do the fore paws in less than a minute.

Adult cats that are not used to being held may struggle
if you try to hold them with there stomach exposed. This
makes them feel very vulnerable. Once a cat feels very
secure she may cooperate in this behavior. In the meantime, put her on your lap and have someone else clip her
nails. Since the forepaws are the offenders in scratching
leave her back claws in tact.

When Is a House Cat an Outside Cat?

Never. But that's not fair to the cat!

If you want your cat to be healthy, safe, and happy, you will create an environment in your house or apartment to provide for her needs. She will look pensively out the window, but it does not mean she should be outside. Your job as her staff is to keep your kitty happy and safe.

Can a house cat ever go outside? Yes, on a leash or in an outdoor enclosure. The outdoor enclosure can be a covered run or large cage in your backyard. If you spend all your spare time gardening, you might want the cat outside with you. With patience you can adapt your cat to a leash and take her on walks.

Leash adjustment may take some time. It starts with a harness of webbing that is flexible and not as interesting to chew as a leather harness. A tiny harness can be fitted to a kitten about four months old. If the harness is too big, take tucks in the straps until she grows into it. You may need to buy a new harness at full growth. Put the harness on her after she has had the opportunity to thoroughly investigate (sniff) it. Most cats are inhibited at first, and will not move around. The cat thinks this is a foreign object and will wait to see what happens. Some cats will immediately start to take the harness off. Always supervise this first experience to make sure your kitty does not get a leg or paw stuck where it should not be. The acquaintance process may be hours or several days. Take the harness off at night or when you're away from home.

When the cat finally understands this is a regular thing, she will ignore it. This is a good time to start the leash process. Attach a piece of cord or string (thick enough that she won't try to chew and swallow it) no more than three feet long, to the D-ring on the harness. Your cat will wonder about the string following her, but again will accept it as normal in time. When she is ignoring the line, take the trailing end and hold it as you follow her around. Do not attempt to direct or control her with it.

The final step is to connect a short, light-weight leash in place of the cord or string. Let her walk around with it. When you want her to stop put gentle pressure on the leash. Do not jerk the cat. Take her on short walks, about 50 feet, and then pick her up, take the harness and leash off, and give her praise and a treat. When she is used to the process, take her outside to a deck or patio for outdoor exploration. Keep the time short, keep the leash in your hand, and carry her back inside before releasing her. One of the most entertaining events in leash training is your kitty's first encounter with grass.

There are some cats that will resist the harness and leash permanently. Keep them indoors and always put them into a travel bag or kennel if they must go outside.

A Cat's-Eye View

DEAR CLYDE,
My Siamese, Osiris, won't stop climbing all over everything, jumping up on the counters, knocking things over, and generally getting into any trouble he can. I've given him toys, but it doesn't help. Why is he being so crazy?

Osiris isn't crazy; he's just bored. Remember, we're predators by nature, and without any kind of real prey to go after, Osiris is just all revved up with no place to go. He needs something to keep him busy, and leaving toys out for him isn't enough. You have to get down on the floor and play with him! We love to play with our humans—we'll even fetch (although don't expect us to bring the toy right back to you like a dog). People think that because we're independent we don't need any attention, like dogs do, and nothing could be further from the truth! So spend a little more time with him and I'll bet he'll knock off the antics.

Kitty Kamp

There are times when humans need to leave home and cannot take the kitty along. Some humans have other humans come to their house and feed the kitty. To a cat, cat-siting means that the human will come in and sit so that the kitty can sit on a lap. Unfortunately many humans are ignorant of this. Sometimes it leads to cat protests which can take the form of a hunger strike, depositing outside of the litter box, or even biting the sitter.

A competent cat sitter is very hard to find. They need to feed her, clean her litter box, watch television with her and read to her. Most cat sitters have not taken the time to understand the full scope of the cat's expectations. And cats can misread the situation, thinking that they have been abandoned to new humans without any say in the matter. Humans have many reasons for their actions and do act without examining all the consequences. Very often the simple solution is to send the cat to kitty kamp.

A good cattery can be an excellent alternative to being left alone. In fact, kitty kamp is fun because there are other cats there. The cattery is usually run by humans that do understand that cats enjoy company sometimes. These humans know that the surroundings are different, the humans are new, and the other cats are unknown. She will have her own room, bowls, and litter box. Perhaps best is the regular routine and attention from the humans. Kitty kamp usually costs more than a cat sitter, but certainly the cat feels she is worth the professional care and the new friends she makes.

If you plan to send your kitty to a cattery, visit it before you bring your pet.

CHECK TO MAKE SURE:

- it is clean and free from odors
- the cages are big enough to permit stretching and climbing
- litter boxes are cleaned and refreshed daily
- the food is provided in a manner your cat is used to
- the counselors spend time with each kitty
- there is an emergency plan in place if your kitty is ill or injured
- each cat has their own cage
- the cage has a scratching post

If you know there will be times when your cat will spend several weeks in a cattery, it is good to have her try it out for just a few days to make sure it is the right choice. If she appears to be stressed, you may need to find another location or another option.

Let's Hit the Road Together

Traveling with your cat should be fun. There are times when you will be faced with difficult situations. Advanced research and some simple tests may help you to avoid those pitfalls.

Traveling by air

Different airlines have different policies and with more pets in more households, the picture is always changing. Most cats, if the airline permits pets, may travel in the passenger cabin because they are small enough to fit into a container that will fit under the seat. The only animals allowed in the cabin uncaged are service dogs. Shipping a cat as cargo has many pitfalls, not the least of which is temperature control. If you must travel by air, go nonstop to your destination, find an airline that has experience with pet passengers, and discuss your plans thoroughly with her vet and the airline personnel.

Traveling by car

This is easiest mode of travel for you and kitty. One requirement planes and cars have in common is the use of a hard container for your cat to ride in. The container needs

to be a familiar place to the cat. It should be purchased well in advance of travel and left open and inviting to your cat. When the cat seems acquainted with it, take her for a short ride. If you only use it when she goes to the vet, it will not be long before she associates needles and probing with the container.

If your cat is a cuddler and wants to be on your lap or shoulder, it means that when you get to a rest stop you can take her out of the container to play. When you are underway, fasten the container securely so it does not shift when you have to apply the brakes. Put your cat's favorite old towel or blanket in the bottom of the container.

Staying at a motel

Staying in a motel can be fun. Check with your local auto association or travel center for information on accommodations that take pets. If you check major motel chains on the Internet, you can find pet policies and fees. Some motels ask for deposits against damage while others actually charge a fee. Their rules usually require that if you leave the room without your pet, that she be in her container in your absence. Some also require that she spend the night in the container. As a courtesy to the motel, if she does sleep on the bed or other furniture, cover it with your personal sheet or blanket. Remember too, that you may be required to stay in a smoking room. If you are using a litter box, take responsibility for cleaning it and disposing of the waste. Do not flush it down the toilet. Do not try to sneak a cat into the motel. They frown on it and will charge you for the indiscretion.

When you arrive at your destination for the night, take her in inside the container. If she is not toilet trained, bring in her litter box along with her food and water bowls. Be sure you have done a recent nail clipping so that she does not damage rugs or furniture. An old hemp or sisal doormat makes a good portable substitute if you are on a long trip.

Staying at a campground

Trips that incorporate camp grounds should be managed the same way as a motel. Many camp grounds will not permit pets of any kind. If they allow them, it could be a container-only arrangement. If there is a leash requirement, be sure kitty is prepared for that eventuality. Your kitty is a house cat and will expect you to provide a litter box, unless she is toilet trained. In a campground setting you need to check the facilities. It may be easier to let her use a litter box on that occasion.

Illness on the road

Pets, just like their humans, can get sick while traveling. Be sure to inquire into available emergency veterinary facilities before setting off on your trip. Larger metropolitan areas generally have an emergency pet facility. If you are going a long distance, check for locations on your route. In rural areas, the veterinary service may be scarce, so plan ahead.

Traveling abroad

Travel in foreign countries can be complicated by all sorts of health requirements for your pet. Be sure that your kitty is current on all her shots. Have a complete set of veterinary records that include those shots. Since you can drive into Canada or Mexico, write, call or email their consulates or embassies for pet requirements. If you have to put your cat in quarantine to enter another country, you may want to leave her at kitty kamp instead.

A Cat's-Eye View

Clyde the cat answers your questions about
SCRATCHING

DEAR CLYDE,
I did just what all of the manuals said and bought a scratching post, but Ruby still scratches the rug! Why won't she use her scratching post?

Is the scratching post covered in carpeting? If it is, look at it from Ruby's point of view—one carpet is just as good as the next, and why shouldn't she use the bigger one that probably allows her to stretch out more? I suggest getting a scratching post that's covered in rope or sisal,

If the post you have isn't covered in carpeting, it's probably not tall enough for Ruby to get any good leverage on it. Try getting a taller post, or getting one of the scratching pads that hangs on a door knob.

Multiple-Pet Households

You have taken the plunge and life with your kitty is wonderful. So now you start wondering, "Can I manage a second cat?" Your first cat is entertaining, very loving, and she has been a friend and so much more. So, if one is good then maybe two will be better. You have the space and the time, so why not?

It is important to remember that cats are very territorial. The cat you already have at home regards it as her home and you are her staff. It may be very difficult for her to learn to share home and staff. In most cases she will come around, but it will take some time.

The best scenario is to introduce a kitten into a household with a mature cat. However, if you are bringing an adult cat into the household, it is best to get a cat that is the same sex and relatively the same size as your first cat, so that she does not feel as threatened. The most important issue is to make sure both cats are spayed or neutered—having to unneutered male cats in one house is a recipe for disaster!

So, how do you handle the introduction of the new play-mate? Here are some guidelines.

A Period of Adjustment

The preparation

Before you put the cats together, give them some adjustment time. As you did with your first cat, give your second cat her own space initially. She will also need her own bowls and litter box. Bring her home in her own travel case, not the one that belongs to your first cat. Let her adjust to you and the surroundings of the one room. Your first cat will be very curious, crying, scratching, and sniffing at the door to the new cat. The newcomer will want to know what is going on as well.

After the new kitty seems comfortable, open the door and block it so that the two cats can see each other but cannot pass through the opening. You might hear great growling and hissing, you might find the new cat hiding away from the door, or you might find the two reaching through the opening in an attempt to make contact. Cats can react in so many different ways; it is wise to continue the separation for awhile.

To advance the information each cat has about her new friend, have them swap space. Put your first cat into the room the new cat is using. She will have plenty to sniff and consider as she examines dishes, the litter box, and anywhere the new scent is found. In the meantime, let the new cat do the same by examining the original cat's bowls and litter box. She is also getting acquainted with the rest of her new home. Make the exchange visits a couple of times so the scent of each cat becomes part of the entire environment.

Once the cats are acquainted, you should still keep separate litter boxes and dishes so that each cat has her own place. You may find they swap bowls and litter boxes all the time or they may be very defensive about "what's mine is mine."

The first meeting

When it is time to introduce the newcomer face to face, hold her on your lap and let the original cat come close to see and sniff. This may elicit growling or hissing. If the original cat just walks away, try putting the newcomer on the floor with her. With both cats on the floor, be prepared for the full range of responses. Watch for the cats to take an aggressive or defensive stance. Remember the aggressor will put her head down, rotate her ears back, close her eyes to slits and draw her lips back. She will hiss and growl and her tail will be lashing on the floor. The defensive cat will be crouched with her ears back and her eyes open. Her mouth may open slightly as she returns the hisses and growls.

If the original cat is the aggressor, try a little longer separation so she gets used to seeing the new cat. If the original cat took the defensive position she may need encouragement from you to make her feel safe. Continue the separation but bring the cats together a couple of times a day. When acceptance begins, maintain the two areas but let the cats roam freely.

If the new cat you bring home is smaller and younger than the original cat, she may feel more vulnerable and is likely to respond by fleeing; or she may decide that this is just another new game. Until you are certain of acceptance keep the two cats separate. Sometimes a bigger or older cat will surprise you by running away from the little cat. This is not unusual if the cat is an only child; she may not know the small animal is another cat. A good sniff should take care of that issue.

Taking the lead

Remember that cats do not adhere to the pack phenomenon which dictates the hierarchy. The cat is territorial, but the tom cat is generally the one that picks fights. Your house cats will have occasional spats, but once they learn to live with each other, they will all, in their own way, take charge.

If you have cats of the opposite sex (both spayed and neutered, of course!), it is common to find the smaller female cat taking over the leadership role. Indeed many households with both female and male cats report that the female cat runs everything. Male cats will hang out together and frequently allow the female to be in control.

What Do You Mean, Another One?

Some humans are pushovers and cats have a way of finding this out. So when you succumb to a third cat, you are playing into their paws.

Start with the same procedure you used with the first two cats. Even after, several weeks, there may be a need for separation. Usually the new cat will be subject to some

hazing. She may get shoved away from her food, or find her litter box is being used by the other two cats. If the situation is very confrontational, you may need to give the new kitty a separate and secure place to eat and use her litter box. Sometimes the third wheel does not fit in until one of the others leaves or another cat comes in to even things up.

With a number of cats in the household, generally the senior female will dominate the behavior and lives of others.

When a roommate leaves

Cats are very aware when one of them is away for an extended time or dies. Cats have routines that involve other cats, and when their routine is disrupted by a missing roommate, they may behave in an unusual way. Searching and constant calling is common in these situations. Some cats may be perceived as grieving; it is possible. The remaining cats will ultimately adjust, but sometimes it takes several months to establish the new routine.

When illness strikes

Having a number of cats is a barrel of monkeys. The downside is health problems and the likelihood of the cats sharing those problems. Be sure your cats are always current on shots and vet visits. Pet health insurance is necessary with multiple cats; check for a multiple cat discount. If one cat is sick, immediately isolate her from the other cats and check with the vet. There is no doubt that you should provide places and toys for all of your cats. They will not necessarily remain organized in your pattern, but the cats will work out the details of the arrangement.

Dogs and Cats

Cats and dogs view their humans quite differently. The dog instinctively responds to a human as part of the pack. He is not sure where he ranks in the pack until the human establishes jurisdiction. Once the dog knows his place, he is content with life. His relationship to other dogs is governed the same way. Often the challenge to become the alpha dog is a fight between an aging alpha and a young aspiring alpha.

Cats work from a different set of instincts. The human in their relationship is a provider and care giver. The dog is not part of the cat's relationship to the human. If the cat determines the dog is friendly and the dog is useful, then the cat will establish a relationship with the dog. She could, however, just as easily ignore him. Do not expect or force the cat and dog to be pals.

Bringing together dogs and cats requires careful planning, but it can result in the two animals having a lasting friendship.

The introductions

Before introducing anything new or different into a cat's domain, think it through. Avoid stressing your cat, as the results can be very unpleasant. Unless you plan to keep your cat and dog totally separate, you will have to plan where each pet will be fed, where the cat litter box will be, and where the cat and dog can each sleep without being disturbed by the other. In this regard, it is difficult to find a place where the dog can sleep that a cat cannot get into. A doghouse or garage where the cat is not permitted may be the best way for the dog to get rest.

Whoever is the first resident is likely to feel extremely territorial about home and humans. Before introducing the new comer it is wise to know its personality and behavior patterns thoroughly. Even a small barking dog will put an adult cat on the defensive. If the dog lives outside and the cat lives inside, you will have fewer problems. Likewise if the dog has been through obedience training, your chances of managing encounters are better.

Dogs are big, noisy and nosy in the eyes of cats. A very large cat such as a Ragdoll or Maine Coon might actually be bigger than a dog. Most dogs want to sniff and check out the cat. Some cats will just walk away rather than be subject to such a personal encounter. Many cats, however, will immediately respond with a hiss, growling, and a sharp claw. Even the biggest dogs are not prepared to have a cat scratch the tender tissue of his nose. A dog understands this type of behavior and probably will relinquish any thoughts of ranking higher than the cat.

Cat-friendly breeds

Before making the decision to bring another animal home, it is important to make sure that the breeds are compatible. There are a large number of dog breeds that get along very well with cats, but there are some that can be problematic. Doing research into the issues you might face can save a lot of headaches down the road.

Spaniels, Schnauzers, Great Danes, and several other breeds have a history of good relationships with cats. That history is not a guarantee, but it is a guideline.

On the other end of the spectrum are terriers, bred to run down small animals, or herding dogs and occasionally dogs trained to protect humans. They have strong instincts just as cats do. If they are left to their own devices, these dogs can terrorize a cat to the point where she has to be completely separated from the household. Stress of that nature is likely to have a permanent effect on the cat.

The best time to bring dogs and cats together is when they are very young. If they are brought together after weaning, puppies and kittens are likely to have a better chance of being playmates as they progress through the puppy and kitten stage. Both of them will achieve adult status at about the same time. but of course there can be a large difference in size. Usually the size will not matter, but be aware that a pair of pets that played well when they were young may unintentionally hurt each other as adults.

The two living together may demonstrate characteristics of each other over time. Your male dog may squat to urinate like a cat. The cat may insist on playing with bones and other dog toys. The dog, being an omnivore, may find nothing wrong with eating his buddy's food. The cat will try to steal off with a good morsel of meat if the dog is not around. Just remember that their needs are different and while occasional sharing is fun, they should not be fed the same food.

The Cat Did It

There can be too many pets in the household. Of course, everyone has seen these stories about someone being turned in to the authorities because she has a zillion cats. Usually, this person has been kind to several cats and then loses perspective and ends up with four or five dozen cats. They are underfed, ungroomed, and most often not spayed or neutered. Removing cats from this sort of life is why rescue and adoption groups are formed. This situation is not the fault of the cat. She stays because there is free room and board, no dogs or kids to tease her, and yes, the place smells horrible but it is better than the alternative. Most humans do not aspire to this and neither do the cats.

Too many pets in your household might number just two. If your pets are aggressive and combative, they provide none of the perks you expected. Caring for pets that create stress will take a huge toll on you. It is important to understand that the personality of a cat is not your fault. The cat has basic instincts and inherited genetic characteristics. When you take her in and communicate how much you like her, she responds. But if early in her life she was ill treated or starved or had to fight just to stay alive, you may not be able to overcome those bad ex-

periences. If you have had experience with cats and want to take on this responsibility, it will be hard work.

You will have to remember that the cat is not mad at you. She has suffered bad treatment and is responding the only way she knows; she's protecting herself. You need to give her safe refuge, and avoid everything that causes her stress. Initially she may resist much contact. Talk to her, feed her, clean her box and spend as much time as possible with her. It may take weeks to get a response. The response might be a soft chirp or purr, or she may give you a quick pass to mark you. She might decide to climb into your lap or into her bed. Keep your voice gentle and movements slow. Pet her gently. If she has been abused she may resist letting you pet some parts of her body. You will have to be very patient. Little treats for good behavior work, but should not be overdone. A cat that has faced starvation is not likely to turn down food. Your kindness could make her fat, and you already have a cat with some problems. Keep her happy, slim and trim.

You are socializing this cat. She will learn to trust you. Her progress will be gratifying but do not assume she is ready for a coming-out party. A relationship with you does not mean a relationship to the rest of the world. With a seriously traumatized cat, allow her to hide when others are present. If you have another human in the household, let the cat determine her relationship to that person. A friend had an older cat that was clearly a one human cat. The cat rejected friends and family. One day a man entered the household and the cat seemed to understand. Although never overtly welcoming, the cat allowed the second human to remain part of the household. Perhaps she was looking for more staff; the man and woman were married.

A Cat's-Eye View

Clyde the cat answers your questions about

GRIEVING

DEAR CLYDE,
After eight years, our cat Cunegonde passed away, and now our other cat, Sabina, has become withdrawn and lethargic. Is she depressed? What can we do to help her?

Some people laugh about this but, just like humans, we definitely do grieve when lose a companion. (interesting tidbit—a cat's brian is more similar to

a human's than a dog's, and both humans and cats have the same exact place in the brain that registers emotion.) Our companions are a big part of our lives and our routines, and when they leave us, our entire life changes and we recognize that. Some of us express our sadness in different ways—we hide, or, sleep too much, or constantly patrol the door or areas where our companions used to hang out, or start meowing excessivly. But it definitely is a grieving process, and it is totally normal.

We grieve anywhere from two weeks to half a year, and we just need our humans to be patient with us. The best thing you can do for Sabina is give her some extra love, and keep her schedule the same (feeding time, etc.). Don't try to drag her out if she wants to be alone, but show her that you care by spending a bit more time with her, and maybe give her a new toy or a few treats. She will be glad for the attention and will come around.

Happiness Is a Healthy Feline

If your cat is healthy and happy, it is not unusual for her to live twenty years—and you want those to be good years. Keeping kitty in good health does not stop at your door. She does need a stress-free environment, nutritious food, adequate sleep, and loving attention. She should look well fed with a full coat of shiny fur, bright eyes with an alert expression, and responsiveness to activity around her. Sometimes, however, she may have a temperature or vomit unexpectedly and need your help.

Veterinarians

Next to you, the most important person in your cat's life is her veterinarian. Even before you bring kitty home, you need to do a little research and familiarize yourself with the veterinary clinics in your area.

Finding the right vet

The best way to find a good veterinarian is to get a recommendation—ask friends who have cats, the local cat rescue groups, or your local Humane Society. Other resources are professional associations that offer listings of veterinarians.

There are several different kinds of veterinary practices. Some will include several doctors and technicians, board and care facilities, and offer a retail outlet for pet supplies; others may be completely holistic. In most major cities you will find an emergency clinic that is open twenty-four hours, and—believe it or not—there are actually veterinarians who actually come to your house. There are times when one is more appropriate to your cat's needs than another. Cats, like humans, have accidents or develop high fevers in the middle of the night, and, knowing how to contact an emergency clinic or drive to their location may just save your cat or kitten.

When you are researching a veterinarian, find out what kind of pets they take care of and what services they offer. Look for clinics with separate waiting rooms for dogs and cats as well as separate treatment and boarding facilities. Kitty, healthy or ill, does not want to be the object of a dog's frenetic barking or lunging.

When you have found good facilities in an accessible location, make an appointment to visit and interview the staff—you will want to know that they are caring, competent, and can communicate with you. Tell them about your plans and ask them specific questions about bringing your kitty home for the first time. If they are service oriented, you should feel comfortable with your choice of clinics and asking your questions. The vet may become a very important person in your new life, so your cat will expect you to be very picky in her behalf.

The first visit

When should your cat have her first visit to the vet? If you acquired a kitten or adult cat that as a stray or foundling, she should be taken to a veterinarian as quickly as possible—try to do it within seventy-two hours of taking her into your home. If you find a cat or kitten, take her to an animal shelter to see if she has an owner.

If you got the cat from a shelter, she most likely has already seen a vet, as immunizing and neutering or spaying are almost automatic with animal shelters. If your kitty has had veterinary care prior to your adoption, ask for her health records. Those records, any information about shots, neutering or spaying, and eating habits, are things you need to know and to tell your new veterinarian.

When you take your cat to the vet for the first time, watch how the vet examines her, how she interacts with her, and what her attitude is about your cat. You want a professional who handles the cat carefully, firmly but with a warm attitude. You do not want the kitten to be afraid of your vet. And, you want the vet to be interested in your kitty and helpful to you so you feel comfortable with the

vet and the kitty. When you choose a doctor for yourself, it is very important to have a level of confidence in your choice. The same is true with the vet. If you have doubts, now is the time to ask questions.

At her first visit, a brand new kitten will be given a schedule of immunizations and when she should have them. This means you will be responsible for taking kitty to the vet at the designated time. By the end of the first year, all the required shots are usually complete so that you will only need annual trips to visit the vet.

I Love Vet Visits

Just having the vet's phone number for emergencies is not the best way to establish your cat's relationship with her vet. You are responsible for making telephone calls and writing down important information. As staff you must make regular appointments for your kitty to visit her vet.

Annual visits to the vet are generally sufficient to update immunization, check weight, heart, blood and her overall health. That may change if your kitty develops a condition such as diabetes which requires regular monitoring. When your cat reaches her senior years, about age, your vet may want to see her semi-annually.

Some staff have discovered that a cat will equate a trip in the travel bag with the vet and shots. To encourage your cat to think more positively about the vet, take her for a visit just to get weighed. Make the visit brief, especially

if you are in a crowded waiting room. When the visit is complete, give her a treat (make it small if she is going on a diet) as a reminder of the pleasant experience. Add in an occasional trip to the drive-thru where she can have a bite of hamburger or chicken.

Most veterinary practices are flexible so that you can make casual visits, have a technician help you weigh the cat or sell you a product that your cat needs. Ask the receptionist or technician the best times for these visits. After a few of these quick visits, the visits that are serious or will involve treatments and shots should be less stressful for kitty and staff.

Identification Tags and Chips

Making sure your cat can be identified if she runs away is very important. Every cat should at least have a collar with identification tags including her address so she can be returned safely. You can find cat-specific collars in any pet store; these collars are made so that they can easily break away if it gets caught, so the cat does not choke.

An alternative to the collar is identification by microchip. This relatively recent technology is used worldwide to identify pet ownership and saves the lives of pets every day. The chip contains information about ownership, including the owner's name, address, and phone number. Municipal shelters and many veterinary clinics are equipped with the scanners to read the chip. There are several systems available in the United States. Even if a

scanner cannot read the specific information, it can determine which system it is in and the shelter can get the appropriate scanner.

Usually veterinarians will chip your kitten when it is about six months old. If your kitten is fairly large, it may be done earlier. The process is quite simple. The fur between the shoulders is quite loose. A hypodermic inserts a tiny chip, about the size of a kernel of pearl barley, under the skin between the shoulders. It stays in that spot for the lifetime of the cat. Whenever a stray is brought to a shelter, one of the first steps is to scan for a chip. If the cat is registered, the owner is contacted.

There is only one place where these systems fail: the human follow up. When you move or change your phone number, it is the human's responsibility to update the information on the chip.

How Does She Tell Me When It Hurts?

Each cat has a pattern and routine of behavior. If she hides for more than a day, misses meals, stops grooming, emits a strange odor, or is abnormally cranky it can be an indication of a health issue or stress issue. It is important to find the cause if the old routine is not reinstated. Unfortunately, she will try to keep you from knowing something is wrong, often by hiding from you. But there are telltale signs that can give you clues as to what is wrong.

A Cat's-Eye View

Clyde the cat answers your questions about
LICKING AND CHEWING

DEAR CLYDE,
Any time I bring home a plastic bag, my little Crisso starts licking it. What gives?

We lick plastic bags because they taste good! I know that sounds silly to humans, but I'll bet you don't know that most plastic bags are made with cornstarch, which can taste pretty good. Some of us just like the texture of plastic bags—they're crinkly, which is fun and feels cool on the tongue. Licking bags is perfectly safe; just make sure Crisso doesn't chew on the bags or swallow any pieces—that could be dangerous.

What is different?

Your cat has very specific routines. She also has a certain appearance. Your first clue that something is different may be ruffled fur or the remnants of breakfast on her whiskers. No two cats are the same and cat staff is the first to notice. Check for clues if you suspect a problem.

If she passes up a meal or seems apathetic about food when you describe her as a "chow hound," this is an abnormal pattern for her. If she stops grooming herself, licks incessantly, or begins to pull out fur, this is an abnormal pattern. If she is lethargic and does not respond to you, her favorite toys, or loud noises, this is an abnormal pattern. Any behaviors that you detect as not typical are cause to examine her. Some clues to look for:

Diarrhea

If you have been cleaning the litter box daily, you know what and when your kitty makes a deposit. Diarrhea is fairly easy to detect and is a symptom of many things. On the less serious side it can be caused by overeating or something new in her digestive tract. On the other hand, the diarrhea can be symptomatic of a variety of serious things: antifreeze poisoning, worms, anaphylaxis, hypothermia, dehydration.

If you have a kitten that has diarrhea, it is important to get help immediately. Whether it is a human, a bovine, or a kitten, diarrhea can cause major dehydration in a relatively short time. The kitten that is just weaned is probably the most vulnerable because she is so tiny. Her thermostat to regulate body temperature is just beginning to work. In this instance you may add hypothermia to the dehydration as the kitten cannot move and generate body heat.

An adult cat should be observed closely; if diarrhea is only a one-time instance and does not show signs of blood, there is less of a threat. If it is more than once, contact the vet. In all cases of diarrhea continue to give the kitty liquids to replenish the system. Remember that a small kitten learns to nurse with her feet under her. When you give her water, do not try to hold her on her back as she may not be able to swallow the liquid. Give her just a drop at a time so she can swallow.

The all-knowing litter box will give more clues to health: worms are common in kittens. The worms come from the mother's body, and often mature in the intestinal tract of the kitten. When round worms are expelled in the feces they look like thin pieces of string or spaghetti. In some instances the kitten will vomit and expel these worms. Some types of worms are virtually invisible. If you suspect worms, take a feces sample to the vet for laboratory analysis.

Vomiting

As with diarrhea, vomiting can be a one time occurrence caused by a new type of food or overeating. One of the most frequent causes of vomiting in an adult is the hairball. Your cat will make it very clear to you if a hairball has caused the vomiting; the evidence is in the cleanup. There are a variety of remedies including specialized cat food, treats and lubricants. Your vet can make a recommendation for your kitty based on her experience. If your cat does not vomit a hairball, she may have swallowed it. Like other situations, this becomes something very different quickly. The cat may appear constipated, off her feed, or lethargic. This problem needs immediate veterinary attention.

If hairballs are not present, look for other causes. Many of those factors—worms, poison, allergic reactions—that cause diarrhea are also responsible for vomiting. The difference is that the dehydration that accompanies vomiting cannot be addressed as easily, as water will likely induce more vomiting. Try to give your cat very small quantities of water—no more than a half ounce—about three times an hour. Cats are finicky at times about temperature, but a thirsty cat might lick an ice cube; a lick or two will help.

Lowered ears

Another indicator of something wrong with your kitty is lowered ears. If your cat's normal ear position is upright and she persists with them lowered and stays in a crouched position, it may indicate she is in pain. It may be caused by something actually wrong with her ears such as an ear infection. If close examination does not reveal discharge, inflammation, or another obvious symptom, there is the chance that the problem is something internal. If the litter box is okay, she appears to be eating normally and she is not vomiting, ask the vet examine her.

Losing her balance

If your cat is walking in circles, carrying her head to one side, and misjudging space, it is quite possible she has an ear infection which has affected her balance. The tiny balancing organs are deep inside the inner ear. An ear infection is very smelly. It may be caused by several different things: fungus, bacteria, or parasites. An infection can cause permanent damage so get kitty into the vet right away.

Feline Illnesses

Cats are subject to many problems similar to humans. They can have diabetes, allergies, obesity, and heart failure. But there are some cat specific problems that are not easily discovered or that develop rapidly.

FELINE LEUKEMIA VIRUS (FLV)

FLV is usually fatal, although not necessarily immediately, and until recently there was no way to control it. There is a vaccine for FLV and will likely be among those the veterinarian recommends for your kitty. Your cat should be immunized before she is exposed to an infected cat. If you have a kitty with FLV it probably will not have a long life, and you should not expose other cats to her.

This is a problem that plagues many male cats. They develop crystals in their urine from its mineral content. The cat's diet and his own genes really are the source of the problem. The crystals form in the bladder and can ultimately block it, preventing the cat from urinating. Recognizing the condition is not easy until the cat has reached a level of serious pain. At that point your cat is not urinating, and the toxins are building up in the blood stream and the kidneys will shut down. The cat will strain to urinate and cry because he cannot. Get immediate attention from the vet to relieve the problem; with a catheter, the pain will lessen and the cat can recover.

Unfortunately, the condition can recur. There is a surgical procedure called a perineal urethrostomy which enlarges the cat's capacity to urinate. The male cat is then able to void in the same manner as a female. If your vet recommends a change in diet, this may be a simpler and less drastic solution to the problem, but the cat will need to be monitored for the likelihood of repetition.

Take her to the vet

The vet is your first resource when the cat communicates that her life is not content. As with human medical care, the vet will make a diagnosis through a variety of techniques. Blood tests and stool and urine samples are a first step for determining what is afflicting your kitty. X-rays may be necessary depending upon the behavior the cat exhibits. There are specialists in veterinary medicine, just as there are in human medicine. If your cat has a serious condition, your veterinarian may suggest having a specialist involved in treatment.

Is She Really Sick?

Sometimes your cat exhibits symptoms that indicate she is sick—she is lethargic, she is not grooming, she will not play, but her temperature is normal, her litter box yields no evidence of diarrhea, and she is not vomiting. There is a very good chance she is feeling stress. Her behavior clearly tells you that she needs help, but what has created the stress and how can you help.

What has changed in the cat's environment? A new puppy in the house could be very upsetting. He is noisy and he gets all the attention from kitty's favorite people. Or the visiting relatives who have a three-year-old girl who tries to take kitty for a ride in her little wagon, dressed in a doll's hat. Last week you decided to paint the bathroom where you keep the litter box. The paint smell is a little strong, but the bathroom looks good. All of these things can create stress in a cat.

Stress can make a cat sick and it can be prevented if you look at it through the cat's eyes. Plans that affect kitty's environment need thoughtful consideration before you go ahead. Are you going on a trip? Where will kitty be and with whom? You have relatives who are coming to visit with their two children. How can you avoid stressing the cat?

Health Insurance

Health insurance for pets is something you should look into when you bring a cat into your home. The cost of health insurance may not be in your plans, but you may need to regroup if your kitty develops health problems. Starting when your kitty first arrives on the scene, pet health insurance can really help. In most programs you will pay the whole amount up front and then send in your paid invoices to get reimbursed. Check with your veterinary clinic and with local shelters. You need to shop for pet health insurance as carefully as you would shop for your own personal health insurance.

How to Avoid CATastrophes and Accidents

CHAPTER 11

- ✦ **STAFF** Responsibilities in CATastrophes
- ✦ **FELINE** First Aid Kit
- ✦ **PLANTS** Are Her Favorites
- ✦ **HOLIDAY** Hazards
- ✦ **POISINING**
- ✦ **CLIMBING**
- ✦ **HOME** Alone
- ✦ **HOW** Hot Is Too Hot

It is difficult to manage CATastrophes and accidents because, hopelessly optimistic staff that we are, we do not think that awful things will happen to us or our darling kitties. To complicate matters, what we think is dangerous doesn't necessarily match what cats see as hazardous. We must pay attention.

Staff Responsibility in CATastrophes

At some point most of us have attended some type of first aid class. It may have been as a kid in the scouts, in your gym class in junior high, or as part of job training. The usual definition of first aid is immediate care so that the victim can sustain life until professional help is available. That is generally the case for cats with a couple of obvious exceptions. A conscious cat cannot explain what happened or where it hurts. Also, the cat hurts and wants to run away. You need to control the cat and at the same time examine her.

Before you do anything to kitty she needs to be restrained. Check with the vet to find out her recommendations for restraint. A small cat or kitten can easily be injured when you are attempting to help something so tiny.

Cats instinctively give up if you grab the scruff—the loose fur at the back of the neck- with one hand and grasp her hind feet with the other. Another form of restraint is to cover the cat's head with a pillow case, holding the case gently at the neck; if the cat is very frightened you may need to pull the pillowcase down to cover her claws. Both techniques will require two people; one to restrain the cat and the other to examine her for the wound or administer aid.

Basic cat-saving skills

Familiar skills in human first aid are part of first aid for your cat. Artificial respiration, CPR, and the Heimlich maneuver can all be performed on a cat, but the procedures have to be done carefully or you can inflict serious harm. As your veterinarian to demonstrate the correct way to do these procedures.

Taking care of a wound

Because a cat tends to hide when it is injured, you might not know there is a wound on your cat. Bleeding generally cleans the wound and coagulates. The problem is that the cat's fur carries dirt that can contaminate a wound. It is important to clear away the fur from a wound. You can

slide two fingers along the skin next to the wound and clip the fur. Do not use electric clippers, as the noise can add more stress to an already stressful situation.

Clean the wound area with cool water, using a sprayer if possible so the water will float away any dirt. After it is clear then spray it with a non-stinging antiseptic solution diluted with water. If you are unsure of the actual damage, leave the wound uncovered and call the vet. If you need to take kitty into the clinic, cover the wound with a non-stick sterile pad and hold it in place with gauze. Use tape to secure the gauze. If you are treating a kitten, contact the vet or the emergency veterinary clinic immediately for instructions.

Getting her to the vet

Wanting to comfort an injured or sick cat is natural for her staff. To protect her from more pain or further injury, transport her carefully in her carrier or a box. Holding her in your arms or even on your lap can be painful for her. If the vet has said that she must be kept still on a rigid surface, use a large bread board or remove a sliding cupboard door or a large cookie sheet and slip it under the cat and then cover her with a towel. Use duct tape or something similar and tape her securely to the board.

Giving kitty her medicine

As much as kitty loves you and you love her, administering medicine can put stress on a beautiful relationship. If you have never given medicine to an animal before, as the veterinarian or vet technician for a demonstration. Cats are rigid and predictable which generally makes them easier to understand. In the case of medicating, this is quite true. Whatever the first experience with medicine it is likely to set the pattern for the rest of the cat's life. As soon as she hears you open the cupboard, get out the bottle, and pick up the syringe, she hides under the kitchen table. The solution will be for you to be less predictable and praise the kitty generously. It may not change the situation, but it will be less stressful.

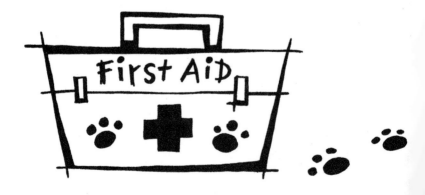

The Feline First Aid Kit

There are some items specifically for first aid for your cat. However, you might not be in a situation where you have access to it and need something immediately. But there are some human remedies that should never be given to a cat:

- ASPIRIN

- LANACANE OR SOLARCAINE

- PEPTO BISMOL OR MYLANTA

- PREPARATION H

- PRESCRIPTION DRUGS

Before giving any human medical remedy to a cat, call your veterinarian and ask if it is all right to give the medicine to the cat and, if so, in what dosage.

Your local pet supply can provide you with a complete first aid kit or you can assemble one yourself. The essentials:

- NEEDLELESS SYRINGE AND PILL GUN
  (FOR ADMINISTERING MEDICATION)

- BLUNT TIPPED SCISSORS OR ELECTRIC CLIPPERS

- NEEDLE NOSE PLIERS (TO REMOVAL OF FOREIGN OBJECTS)

- TWEEZERS FOR SLIVERS ARE GENERALLY IN THE HOUSE, SOMEWHERE!

- BANDAGES, TAPE, AND ELASTIC BANDAGES

- RECTAL THERMOMETER OR DIGITAL THERMOMETER

- COLD AND HOT PACKS OR HOT WATER BOTTLE

- BETADINE SOLUTION

- CALAMINE LOTION

Taking kitty's temperature

This is a skill you should master. Temperature elevation is an indicator of many things; it should be checked if you have seen any deviation from her normal routine. Lubricate the tip of a rectal thermometer with petroleum jelly. Put kitty on a counter with your left arm around her, pulling her to your chest and let her head rest on your elbow. If she is frightened or very feisty, wrap a towel around her to protect yourself. Lift the base of the cat's tail with your left hand, and use your right hand to slowly insert the thermometer about a half inch into the rectum. Talk to her softly throughout the procedure to reassure her. Leave it for three minutes and then remove it. The normal cat temperature is between 100.4 and 102.5 degrees. Any higher reading requires a call to the vet. If you have a digital thermometer, follow the manufacturer's instructions or check with the vet.

Plants Are Her Favorites

Cats come with a normal curiosity, and they recognize plants as a source of moisture. It isn't unusual to find teeth marks in any kind of plant matter. Nor is it unusual to find your cat going back to the plants regularly even if it causes her to vomit. If you enjoy plants and flowers in your home, you need to exercise caution about which plants you select.

There are more than 700 plants identified as harmful to pets. The Humane Society of the United States has produced a list that you can find on their website. Some of those most likely to be in your house as cut flowers or potted plants are included here.

Unsafe

- IRIS
- DELPHINIUM
- LILY OF THE VALLEY
- NARCISSUS
- PHILODENDRONS
- DAFFODILS
- RHODODENDRON

- YELLOW OLEANDER
- AUTUMN CROCUS
- AZALEAS
- BIRD OF PARADISE
- CASTOR BEAN
- AFRICAN VIOLETS
- ORCHIDS

Safe

- BEGONIAS
- BACHELOR BUTTONS
- SNAPDRAGONS
- CANNAS
- CAMELLIAS
- SWORD FERN
- HENS&CHICKENS

- GLOXINIA
- VENUS FLYTRAP
- JASMINE
- ZINNIA
- ICE PLANT

Holiday Hazards

Holiday plants are among the most frequent problems because a cat who does not see much in the way of plants will be very curious about strange things you introduce into her environment. Mistletoe, Poinsettia, and the Christmas rose, are popular and even if you don't purchase them friends may bring them to your home as gifts. If you can display them in a cat proof location, outside on the deck, that is wonderful. If they cannot be safely displayed, find a new home for them where there are no pets. If you always put up a real Christmas tree, be sure that the water in the stand sits is covered so that kitty will not use it as watering hole.

Easter lillies are popular in the spring with huge flowers and a strong fragrance. Any part of this plant is toxic to cats. You might mention to your friends prior to the holidays that you have problems with plants that appeal to the cat. If they do not take the hint, be more straightforward or hide the plants from the cat until you can safely dispose of them.

Poisoning

There are poisoning hazards other than plants all over your house. Removing them from the cat's environment is the best way to avoid her being poisoned.

Chocolate is one of the most dangerous foods for a cat. It is chock full of theobromine, a stimulant that affects the heart. The darker the chocolate, the more theobromine. Chocolate is also a diuretic, and can result in diarrhea, lethargy, vomiting, depression, and muscle tremors. If kitty decides to lick the ice cream dish after you finish, there is little likelihood of the chocolate ice cream causing illness. Nevertheless, keep chocolate stored where the cat can't get to it.

Antifreeze has been mentioned several times because it is sweet, and something we keep around to use in our cars. If your cat appears to have been poisoned by drinking the antifreeze, deal with it the same way as for chocolate.

What to do

If the cat has been poisoned but is conscious and in control (not having seizures) you need to make her vomit. Before you try to make her vomit, give her a small meal or treat which will make vomiting easier and less irritating.

After she has swallowed the treat, give her a small dose of 3% hydrogen. Use an eye dropper or needleless syringe to get the liquid at the back of her tongue. Use no more a teaspoon or two for every ten pounds of body weight. If she does not vomit, repeat the procedure after five minutes. If she does not respond after three tries get her to the vet right away.

There is a product is called ToxiBan, a liquid-activated charcoal that can be used to make a cat vomit. It tastes terrible, and it is a struggle to get them to take it. Ordinarily a vet would be the one to use it. If you are not handy to a vet, then try giving it to her. Do not give your cat ipecac.

If your cat ingests something that is caustic, do not make her vomit. The tissue has already been irritated by the acids and alkalis. Give her bread soaked in olive oil. It will be less of an irritant and absorb some of the material she swallowed. Often the caustic materials burn the tender tissue around and inside the mouth. Spritz it with water or milk. Then get her to the vet immediately.

The same treatment will be necessary if your cat swallowed a petroleum product. You do not want her to vomit as the petroleum may get into her lungs. As with the caustic products, the bread and oil will coat the digestive system and serve to absorb some of the material.

If you suspect poisoning, contact the ASPCA National Animal Poison Control Center which is a twenty-four-hour, seven-day service that can assist you. You will find them in the reference section.

A Cat's-Eye View

Clyde the cat answers your questions about

BAD BEHAVIOR

DEAR CLYDE,
I'm going crazy—my cat Georgie will pee in his litter box, but he poops in the bathtub! What is his problem?

There's nothing wrong with Georgie—he's just a neat-freak, although you probably don't think so because he's messing up your bathroom. Georgie's doing this because he's already used the litter box to pee in and he wants a clean place to do his other business - and what could be cleaner than your tub?

I can't stress it enough, people—we need clean litter boxes! Keep on top of Georgie's litter box, and I'll bet you good money he'll stop using the bathtub.

Climbing

The first time your kitten takes to the air it will be scary, entertaining, and enlightening. With instincts to hunt, take flight, and basic curiosity in full bloom, she will learn quickly. Cats and kittens are not unfamiliar to the local fire department, police department, and the power company. Climbing up is taking flight from something. When the cat finally feels safe, she stops and looks around. She finds herself in more trouble because she is now high in a tree, and needs to get down. She knows the best way to get down is to call for help. Her cries will be heard throughout the neighborhood. Adult cats usually figure it out and get themselves down. For a kitten this is all new and she may stay in the tree all night hoping for help. You or someone will have to fetch her down.

Cats do not stop climbing just because they live indoors. The difference is that you will not have to embarrass yourself in public while trying to keep your cat from dare devil tricks. Cats love high shelves. The top of the bookcase is nice and the top of the kitchen cabinets is great. The very high shelf in the linen closet is perfect for a good nap because she won't be disturbed. The loft-style home with balconies over a living area is especially spectacular when it comes to adventure. Kitty can sit watching the action without detection until she leaps for the light fixture, hanging basket planter, or the floor to ceiling drapes on the opposite wall.

If you find that your cat really is a climber, do not assume that she will always be successful. It is not unusual for a cat to jump or fall from amazing heights, but it is

not worth grief it could cause. If she falls from a shelf or ledge while young it is possible to break a bone or do internal organ damage. This possibility needs to be eliminated. If you have the space, create an area designated for climbing and thrill seeking by covering it with carpet or can install a floor to ceiling scratching post that is safe to climb and leap from, or buy a ready-made cat condominium at the pet store.

Is she hurt?

Cats easily make jumps from six feet or more, but a fall of that distance can be very dangerous. If you do not see a fall, there are ways to determine if your cat has been hurt. When cats limp or refuse to move at all it may mean a broken bone or internal injury. If she will not eat, it may indicate an injury to face, teeth or jaw. Difficulty breathing is another symptom of a possible fall. The hardest part of determining damage is the fact that she may have serious internal injuries and you cannot detect it. It does happen that actual problems may not surface for an hour or so. Get immediate help.

If the fall results in bleeding or an open wound, it is important to control the bleeding. Use a gauze pad to apply direct pressure. The bleeding generally will cease in five minutes. If you are not sure if the bleeding is continuous, do not lift the pad; keep it in place and add another if it seems necessary. If the wound is open, cover it with a clean towel and get help quickly. For an abdominal wound, wrap plastic wrap around her chest to seal it and make transport safer. Use a sheet long enough to wrap around her body and lap over the other edge.

Home Alone

When you were a kid, and your mom and dad were at work or shopping, did you ever snoop in all those places that your folks would not let you into? Well, when you leave the cat at home alone she is very busy. She uses this opportunity to get into places you might not approve. She probably prowls at night while you are sound asleep. Skills such as opening sliding doors are honed during these long absences so she has ready access to all sorts of cat food.

One thing she discovers and keeps to herself is hiding places. Finding a new den to rest and groom is a wonderful adventure. When you call her she often ignores you and stays put. It becomes your job to find her in her new spot. As she discovers new spots she also discovers the location of your sweater collection, which are great for chewing, heavy coats perfect for great scratching, and old leather shoes, which have a smell that many cats find irresistible.

If you hide poison for ants or mice, the several hours alone can give kitty enough time to find those items. Do you remember where you placed those things? It is important to make sure they are not in kitty's den.

How Hot Is Too Hot?

Although we think that cats can handle warmer temperatures, it is always a difficult situation if they get too warm. A cat's coat helps to keep them cool. If they have not been groomed, the coat is matted and air cannot circulate. The cat grooms herself during hot weather in part so that the evaporating saliva is helping with the cooling process. Under normal conditions, even long-haired cats can stay cool if they get a helping hand.

If a cat is so warm that she is panting, she is already in the danger zone. First, take her temperature; if it is above 106 degrees, get her to the vet immediately.

If her temperature is below 104 degrees she may have moderate heat stroke. You need to take steps to cool her. If you have air conditioning put her inside with the AC on high. If your house is not air conditioned, turn on the AC in your car and stay with her until she is better. If you have no air conditioning at all then use a fan to improve evaporation. You can use ice and alcohol on the cat's groin and in her armpits to help with cooling as will placing her in front of the air vent to facilitate evaporation. Putting her in a sink or tub of cool water will also help (be sure to keep her head above water). Give her cold water or some ice chips to lick. When her temperature is down to 103 degrees stop the process to keep her from a chill. Let her rest quietly in the shade.

CHAPTER 12

The CATalog

It is extremely important to keep detailed records for felines. As you have discovered, cats connect things as they happen and they are good at recalling routine. It is your job to recall the many little details of her life.

There are spaces in this log for almost everything. Because every cat is different, you will find some extra spaces to write about those things only you and your cat know.

❧ **Birth date and location**

❧ **Address, phone, email**

EMERGENCY INFORMATION

❧ **Vet's name, address and phone**

❧ **Emergency clinic phone, local animal control, pharmacy**
Animal Poison Control Center 1-888-426-4435

❧ **Taxi or emergency transport to phone number,
driving directions to emergency clinic**

All About

-- (cat's name)

and Me

(paste mug shots here)

Cat Stats

❧ **Age**

❧ **Sex**

❧ **Breed**

❧ **Weight**

❧ **Normal Temperature**

❧ **Respirations**

❧ **Abnormalities, disabilities**

❧ **Allergies**

❧ **Cat Astrological Information**

❧ **Cat's Favorite Playmate(s)**

❧ **Cat's Best Friend**
(after you, of course)

❧ **Cat Purrreferences**

FOOD AND WATER

❧ **Type of Food and Brands**

❧ **Storage Location**

❧ **Feeding Schedule**

❧ **Feeding Station Location**

❧ **Additional Water Stations**

❧ **Snacks and Treats**

LITTER

❧ **Brand of Litter preferred**

❧ **Storage Location**

❧ **Disposal Plan**

❧ **Box Locations**

NAPPING SCHEDULE

- **Early AM**

- -

- **Post Eating**

- -

- **Late AM**

- -

- **Early PM**

- -

- **Post Exercise**

- -

- **Mid PM**

- -

- **Post Dinner, Lap Nap**

- -

- **Bedtime**

- -

- **Napping Locations**

- -

- -

- **Secret Locations**

- -

- **Favorite Blanket**

- -

+ **Favorite Pillows**

+ **Favorite Lap Locations**

FAVORITE TOYS (ROTATE TO AVOID BOREDOM)

+ **Favorite Non-Toy Toys** (she will help you find these:
  paper bags, empty boxes, spools, straws, wads of paper, etc.)

+ **Catnip Stash Location**

+ **Favorite TV (window with shelf)**

GEAR

- **Athletic Gear** – leash, harness, ping pong balls,
- **Travel Gear** – cat bag, cat hard carrier, travel dishes

HEALTH

- **Immunization Record** (annual/monthly)

- **Visits to the Vet** (notes, future dates)

- **Teeth Cleaning**

MISCELLANEOUS

❧ **Gift Ideas**

❧ **Toy Shops**

❧ **Pet Supply**

❧ **Websites**

❧ **Purchases/dates/likes & dislikes/cost**

❧ **Favorite Drive-Thru Food**

❧ **Preferred Kitty Kamp** (boarding, cattery)

❧ **TV Shows – Daytime**

Bibliography

AAA. *Traveling With Your Pet*, 3rd edition. Heathrow, Florida: AAA Publishing, 2001.

Brotman, Eric, Ph D. *How to Toilet Train Your Cat: The Education of Mango*. San Fernando, California: Bird Brain Press, Inc, 2000.

Kunkel, Paul. *How to Toilet Train Your Cat: 21 Days to a Litter-Free Home*. New York: Workman Publishing, 1991.

Shojai, Amy D., DVM. *First- Aid Companion for Dogs and Cats*. USA: Rodale Inc, 2001.

Reference Websites

Microchip

WWW.AKCCAR.ORG
This registry is run by the AKC but takes all companion pets. It has just come out with a new microchip.

WWW.AVIDMICROCHIP.COM
a manufacturer and maintains a registry.

WWW.HOMEAGAIN.COM
a registry and also provides other emergency info.

WWW.24PETWATCH.COM
a registry and also provides other services.

Cat Associations/ Registries

WWW.ACFACATS.COM
American Cat Fanciers Association, founded in 1955

WWW.CFAINC.ORG
Cat Fanciers Association, founded in 1906

WWW.CFFINC.ORG
Cat Fanciers Federation, covers Northeast USA

WWW.TICAEO.COM
The International Cat Association, largest genetic registry

WWW.TRADITIONALCATS.COM
Traditional Cat Association, founded 1987

National Animal Protection

WWW.ASPCA.ORG
American Society for
the Prevention of Cruelty
to Animals

WWW.HSUS.ORG
Humane Society of the
United States, great source

Cat Welfare/Rescue

WWW.21CATS.ORG
21Cats

WWW.ALLEYCAT.ORG
Alley Cat Allies

Veterinarians

INFO@AAFPONLINE.ORG
American Association of
Feline Practitioners

WWW.AVMA.ORG
American Veterinary Medical
Association

Emergency

WWW.ASPCA.ORG or
1-888-426-4435 Animal Poison
Control Center 24/7

Supplies

WWW.SOFTPAWS.COM
acrylic covers for your cat's claws

WWW.BONAFIDO.COM
soft recovery collars for your cat
(foam)

WWW.ARCATAPET.COM
soft recovery collars for your cat
(cloth)